Plain Thoughts

Also from Westphalia Press
westphaliapress.org

Plain Thoughts on Secret Societies

by John Lawrence

WESTPHALIA PRESS
An imprint of Policy Studies Organization

Westphalia Press
An imprint of Policy Studies Organization
1527 New Hampshire Ave., NW
Washington, D.C. 20036
info@ipsonet.org

ISBN-13: 978-1-63391-213-7
ISBN-10: 1633912132

Cover design by Taillefer Long at Illuminated Stories:
www.illuminatedstories.com

Daniel Gutierrez-Sandoval, Executive Director
PSO and Westphalia Press

Updated material and comments on this edition
can be found at the Westphalia Press website:
www.westphaliapress.org

PLAIN THOUGHTS

ON

SECRET SOCIETIES.

BY

JOHN LAWRENCE.

I SPAKE OPENLY TO THE WORLD, AND IN SECRET HAVE I SAID NOTHING......BUT
HE THAT DOETH TRUTH COMETH TO THE LIGHT.   Jesus Christ.

BE NOT CONFORMED TO THIS WORLD......WHAT COMMUNION HATH LIGHT WITH
DARKNESS ?   Paul.

PREFACE.

The continued demand for "Plain Thoughts," makes it necessary that we immediately issue this *Fifth Edition*, four editions having already been exhausted; and we are fully satisfied, from our own examination and the concurrent opinions of many excellent persons who have read the work, including quite a number of unimpeachable character who have had a long practical connection with leading secret societies, that it exhibits in a clear, truthful and forcible manner, the character and claims of Secret Associations. The subject is discussed lucidly, candidly, and in a spirit so kind and christian, that no person can, with any good reason, be offended at it. It is indeed a book of "plain thoughts," so expressed as to be easily understood. Every important position assumed, is sustained by ample evidence drawn from entirely reliable sources. In all questions of fact respecting any secret order, the standard writings of members of the order in question are adduced. It is a main object of the book to prove that all secret orders are opposed to the spirit of true religion,—are really deistical in character,—and the position which a christian should maintain respecting them, is presented in the clear light of the Divine word.

Since the first edition was issued in 1852, quite a number of new secret societies have thrust themselves upon the attention of the public, and have become exceedingly bold and clamorous in urging their claims; and one of them in particular has attempted to assume the management of our government, and to decide in the lodge who shall rule; but the fundamental principles of all these new secret creations, are identical with the principles of the older societies, and the general argument of this work, proves that those principles are unsound, unsafe, unchristian, and necessarily evil, and ought to be discarded by all good men. We copy below a few

NOTICES OF THE RELIGIOUS PRESS.

The "*New York Evangelist*" says :—"It is a pointed and decisive blow at those undefensible and doubtful associations."

The "*Oberlin Evangelist*" says :—"It is fearless, outspoken, sensible, and not wanting in thoroughness of discussion. It is addressed to christians, with christian arguments, and manifestly with a desire to do good.   *   *   We advise both the advocates and opponents of secret societies, to get and read the book.   *   *   We hope this book will help forward an earnest, christian discussion of the subject in hand."

The "*Wesleyan Expositor*" says :—"We have read this book with much satisfaction. It is what the title imports, Plain Thoughts well and plainly expressed ; and cannot fail to do good. We would feel that we were doing a good work in selling it. It ought to have an extensive circulation."

Similar notices have appeared in the "*Presbyterian of the West*," "*Christian Press.*" "*Golden Rule.*" "*Wesleyan.*" "*Presbyterian Advocate*," etc., but we have not space to insert them here.

THE PUBLISHERS.

Contents.

CHAPTER I.

ANTIQUITY OF SECRET SOCIETIES.

CHAPTER II.

ARGUMENTS AGAINST ALL SECRET SOCIETIES.

CHAPTER III.

THE SAME SUBJECT CONTINUED.

CHAPTER IV.

OATHS OF FREEMASONRY.

CHAPTER V.

ADAMS' LETTER TO EDWARD LIVINGSTON.

CHAPTER VI.

MISCELLANEOUS OBJECTIONS TO FREEMASONRY.

CHAPTER VII.

SONS OF TEMPERANCE.

CHAPTER VIII.

BENEVOLENCE OF SECRET SOCIETIES.

CHAPTER IX.

CHRISTIAN CHARITY.

CHAPTER X.

CONNECTION OF CHRISTIANS WITH SECRET SOCIETIES.

CHAPTER XI.

ARGUMENTS AND OBJECTIONS ANSWERED.

CHAPTER XII.

INTRODUCTORY.

THERE is no wrong principle which we should be afraid to oppose, however popular or powerful it may be; and there is no right principle which we should shrink from supporting, however few or weak its advocates. When a principle is proposed for adoption, among the various inquiries which it is proper to make, there is one, unquestionably paramount to all others, viz: IS IT RIGHT? If a social organization is proposed, and you are invited to enter into it, and spend time, money and labor in it, this question never should be forgotten: Is the organization established upon right principles? Will it bear the ordeal of the Word of Truth? Will it please God?

Men, who seriously reflect but little, and have little conscience and less faith, are not very scrupulous about the *right* or *wrong* of a question; but, with them, the inquiry of paramount importance is, Will this principle, if advocated, or this organization, if patronized, contribute to my personal interest?

Selfishness is the luxuriantly corrupt soil in which innumerable evils grow with marvelous rapidity; and yet, who will affirm that it is the soil in which secret societies all take root and grow? The author of this book believes that all secret associations *are* purely selfish in their organizations,—that the corner-stone of each and all is selfishness; and that, although they may appear to accomplish good, their ultimate tendency, taken all together, is "evil, only evil, and that continually."

It would be unwise and rash to say that honest men were not found connected with these secret fraternities; but that they have no tendency to make men good, to elevate the mind, sanctify and ennoble the heart, but on the contrary, to darken and degrade it, is honestly believed. Some may withstand this deleterious influence, but the large majority will gradually sink into the dead level of selfishness, which is the basis of such combinations.

We do not come before the public as a personal enemy of the members and advocates of secret societies, by no means; for we have no feelings of personal ill-will to any man, or set of men; and it would be exceedingly painful, if an honest expression of sentiment on an important subject should be construed into an intention to inflict personal injury. We do not oppose *men*, but principles. To secret societies, and not to men, we are undisguisedly unfriendly.

No reasonable person will say a man has not a right to publish a book against these orders, because they are writing continually in vindication of them selves. They are publishing numerous papers, periodicals, and books, designed to persuade men to enlist under their banners; and surely it would evince a pusillanimous spirit indeed, for them to

fall out, because a book or pamphlet against their
views should make its appearance.

We must say, however, that a disposition has
been manifested, in certain quarters, to suppress
opposition by other and less honorable means than
facts and *arguments*. Personal insults have been
offered to some who have spoken and written plainly,
and they have been told that they need not expect
to prosper in business, if they are not silent. In
other words, it is more than hinted that these fra
ternities will bring a secret power to bear upon
individual opposers. We resent with scorn any
such intimidations. We always hated, but never
feared, a secret inquisition, however unfair and
devilish a secret attack upon an individual is.

We do not intend to bring out a revelation of the
hidden glories or concealed shame, the profound
wisdom or profounder nonsense, of secret societies.
Not at all. We have never been blessed with a
connection with any such. To our mind secrecy

has possessed no charms; and we do not even desire to look into the astonishing manifestations of excellence said to be in the lodge-room, unrevealed to the vulgar crowd. We have never quizzed a Mason, an Odd Fellow, or a Red Man, in order to find out *something;* and we are perfectly contented to live and die in profound ignorance of all the sublime nothings preserved with such scrupulous care and exclusiveness. There are at least a few scattering truths to be learned outside of lodge-rooms. And we have never been very powerfully impressed with the striped, spotted or speckled garments, whether of green, white, black, or blue, and all the silly and childish regalia, together with the empty dignities so profusely conferred by all these orders. These are good for nothing but to dazzle the minds of simpletons.

We shall write in straight-forward English, adducing facts and arguments, not always in graceful, but, we trust, in plain style, so that the meaning will be readily apprehended. We write to do good.

If any see proper to become offended because an humble individual takes liberty to write freely, we respectfully request them, beforehand, to get into a pleasant temper again as soon as they can, so that the sun may not go down upon their wrath.

There are thousands of conscientious and sound-minded men who are opposed to the admission of secret fraternities into the social organization; and there are thousands of respectable Christians who regard connection with secret societies as religiously wrong. These all have a right to think, to write, and to speak. We claim this natural right, and ask only to be heard with candor.

PLAIN THOUGHTS.

I.

Antiquity of Secret Societies.

THERE is a disposition in the human mind to venerate whatever bears the rust of antiquity or wears the venerable robes of old age ; and it is considered in some quarters sufficient evidence of the sacredness of a thing, that it is ancient. Hence it is thought almost sacrilegious to utter a word against a society which has been patronized for centuries. A man would once have been pronounced an infidel and impious, if he had said that ancient Rome was not founded by the gods. We admit we should reverence age and reflect before we differ.

Secret societies wear the honors of age. They are old as Christianity,—old as the

Roman and Grecian Republics,—as old, perhaps older than civil history. Some accounts of them are found in the most ancient records, though no one has yet, we believe, traced their origin to heaven; and indeed their general character betrays their earthly origin, and the sublunary soil out of which they have grown. These societies are usually connected with religion—the religion of the countries in which they flourish—and assume a kind of sacredness, which is concealed from the public eye, in part, so as to produce awe in the minds of the uninitiated.

Such was the character of ancient secret societies. The worship of the god Bacchus was brought out of Egypt to Athens; and connected with his worship there were certain mysteries, into which the Athenians might be " initiated." Those who were connected with these mysteries, appeared before the public on certain great days with fantastic dresses or regalia, which were designed to impress the gazing throng with astonishment. We will introduce a few historical notices. Rollin says:

" Those who were *initiated* mimicked whatever the poets thought fit to feign of the god Bacchus. They covered themselves with the skins of wild beasts; carried a thyrsus in their hands—a kind of pike, with ivy leaves twisted around; had drums, horns, pipes and other instruments calculated to make a great noise; and wore upon their heads wreaths of ivy and vine branches, and other trees sacred to the god Bacchus."

Of another society, called by way of eminence " The Mysteries," the same historian says:

" When the time for their initiation arrived, they were brought into the temple; and to inspire the greater reverence and terror, the ceremony was performed in the night. Wonderful things took place on those occasions. Visions were seen and voices were heard of an extraordinary kind. A sudden splendor dispelled the darkness of the place, and disappearing, added new horrors to the gloom. Apparitions, claps of thunder, earthquakes, heightened the terror and amazement; whilst the person to be admitted, overwhelmed with dread, and sweating through fear, heard trembling the mysterious volume read to him, if in such a condition he was capable of hearing at all. These *nocturnal* rites gave birth to many disorders, *which the severe law of silence, imposed on the persons initiated,* prevented from coming to light, as Gregory Nazianzen observes."

It is worthy of special remark here, that Socrates, the "divine philosopher," refused to connect himself with this organization. Rollin says, "he would not be initiated into those mysteries, which was, perhaps, one reason which rendered his religion suspicious."

We select from the celebrated Mosheim the following :

"But beside the public worship of the gods, to which all without exception were admitted, certain rites were practiced in secret by the Greeks, and several eastern nations, to which a very small number had access. They were commonly called *mysteries;* and the persons who desired to be initiated therein were obliged previously to exhibit satisfactory proofs of their fidelity and patience, by passing through various trials and ceremonies of the most disagreeable kind. These secrets were kept in the strictest manner, as the initiated could not reveal anything that passed on those occasions without exposing their lives to the most imminent danger; and that is the only reason, at this time, we are so little acquainted with the true nature and real design of those hidden rites."

From the incomparable History of the Christian Religion and Church by the celebrated *Neander*, we extract the following:

"It well nigh seems as if he (Philo) found cause to warn his fellow believers against the fascinations of mystery, by which they also could be attracted. All mysteries, (says he) all parade and trickery of that sort Moses removed from the holy giving of the law; since he did not wish those who were trained under such a form of religious policy to be exposed by having their minds dazzled by mysterious things, to neglect the truth, and to follow after that which belongs to night and darkness, disregarding what is worthy of light and of the day. Hence no one of them that know Moses, and count themselves among his disciples, should allow himself to be initiated into those mysteries or to initiate others; for both the learning and the teaching of those mysteries is no trifling sin. For why, ye initiated, if they are beautiful and useful things, do ye shut yourselves up in profound darkness, and confer the benefit on two or three alone, when you might confer it on all, were you willing to publish in the market place what would be so salutary to every one, so that all might certainly partici- pate of a better and happier life? He points to the fact that in the great and glorious works of nature there is no mystery, all is open. He bears witness to the mere empty mechanism into which mysteries had then degenerated; men, he says, of the worst character and crowds of abandoned women were initiated for money."

From these quotations it is evident that secret societies, though not of a very respect- able character, existed when Athens flourished as an infant Republic—yea, ancient Egypt was the theatre of their operations, and we may add, probably the place of their birth. Their dress or regalia is described; their imposing public processions, and the one thing essential to all such organizations is stated, viz: the strongest obligations *to conceal the secrets* of their orders. Non-divulgence was an *essential* law. Their meetings, like those of all secret associations, were at night, and only the initiated could be present, and they dared not tell what passed to the uninitiated. Says Rollin: "These nocturnal rites gave birth to many *disorders, which the severe law of silence imposed on the persons initiated prevented from coming to light.* Says Mosheim: "*These secrets were kept in the strictest manner, as the initiated could not reveal anything that passed on those occasions without exposing their lives to the most imminent danger!*"

Those, evidently, were secret societies in full credentials! Those who entered were bound to reveal nothing that passed, and the penalty annexed to this law of silence was death! Great disorders existed, yet no one dared bring them to light! We also learn from the above historical notices that the plain, humble, open-hearted *Socrates*, who loved the common people and sought only to do good, "would not be initiated," and that Philo, the learned Jewish Philosopher, warned the disciples of Moses against the fascinations of these societies, considering the learning and teaching of their mysteries a great sin.

It is also evident from the sacred scriptures that at the period of the establishment of Christianity secret associations existed; and they were then probably at the zenith of their glory or their shame. Of them the Apostle to the Gentiles speaks in terms of earnest warning: "And have no fellowship with the unfruitful works of darkness, but rather reprove them. For it is a shame even to speak of those things which are done of them in secret." Ephes. 5: 11, 12.

These secret societies or mysteries, at the time the apostle wrote, flourished all over heathendom, and were exceedingly powerful. The apostle declares their works of darkness to be unprofitable, and so shameful that modesty would blush at their recital. He tells his Christian brethren to have *no fellow-*

ship with them, and it is a fact worthy of regard, that wherever the cross was triumphant, the power of these societies fell, prostrated and destroyed. We might quickly decide, as did the apostle, that there could be no affinity, fellowship or brotherhood between Christianity and secret societies.

The FREEMASONS' *claim to Antiquity.*—The fraternity of Freemasons puts in a strong claim to a very high antiquity. It is boldly asserted that King Solomon was a Freemason, and an eminent patron of the order —that all those workmen mentioned in 2 Chron., 2d chap., were Masons, and that several kings of Israel and Judah were Masons. They number in the list of brothers and patrons, numerous prophets, apostles and saints. John the Baptist, the harbinger of the blessed Jesus; and John the Evangelist and Revelator, who was with the Redeemer on the Mount when his " divinity burst through his humanity," and on the sea-girt Patmos, it is unblushingly affirmed, were eminent patrons of speculative Freemasonry. If the forerunner of Christ and his beloved disciple were eminent Masons, is it unreasonable to suppose they would have initiated their Master? Now here we have, according to Masonic legend, the plain, honest, holy Baptist and the single-hearted Evangelist transformed into Freemasons, with the blasphemous inference that Jesus Christ was himself a Freemason!

But where is the evidence of all these high claims? Where is the reliable history sustaining these assertions. A masonic friend replies, "Evidence! do you ask for *historical* evidence? such as would sustain other facts before sensible men? We cannot give you such, but we have any quantity of legend and tradition! You must believe Masonry without evidence!" Ah, indeed! we shall not do that; we ask for *evidence, testimony, witnesses*. Where are they? Echo, from every lodge room, answers, *legend, tradition, say-so!*

"But Solomon was a Mason." Where is the evidence? Do the inspired books of Kings and Chronicles mention such a fraternity? "Ah, yes," exultingly answers my masonic friend, "we read of Masons who were employed in the erection of Solomon's temple!" This is a grand argument indeed! The men who quarried, dressed and laid stone in the temple of the Lord, speculative Freemasons!—a secret, oath-bound fraternity. This is a dizzily absurd position. We as reasonably might assert that the stone masons who built the pyramids of Egypt were speculative Freemasons. And, to climax the absurdity, that every man who laid a brick or stone in ancient Nineveh, Babylon or Memphis, or that helped to carve an obelisk or turn an arch, was a speculative Freemason, initiated into the sublime mysteries, and sworn to conceal, through life, on penalty of death, the secrets of the order!

But to return to the temple of Solomon. It would be as reasonable to assert that the *hewers of wood* and *carpenters* were secret, oath-bound societies, and that Solomon belonged to the fraternity of *Free Hewers* and *Free Carpenters!* That the prophets were Free Carpenters! That John the Baptist, and John the Revelator were Free Carpenters!

Away with such absurdity, you say. I reply, it rests upon the same vain suppositions that the masonic pretensions rest upon, and has as much evidence in its support.

But what does John the Baptist say about Freemasonry? Let us see. He writes of repentance, baptism, reformation, the coming of Christ, &c., but not one word about Masonry. And John the Revelator, what has he to say? He wrote five books of the Scriptures, but not one word about Free-masonry. And *there is not a particle of evidence that any patriarch, prophet, king of Israel, apostle or evangelist, ever knew anything about this secret society.* All that has been so finely said about masonic prophets and Bible saints are fictitious inventions of modern times, designed to deceive the ignorant, and beg an influence from those worthy men; and are as unworthy of credence as the stories of *Sinbad the sailor* or old *Blue Beard.* How grave ministers of the gospel can repeat them again and again as truths, is marvelous to us. We would be no more surprised and disgusted to hear a Rev. gentleman read a chapter about

Aladdin and the wonderful lamp as sacred truth.

Let it be remembered, that, first, there is not a shadow of evidence that Freemasonry existed in ancient times, though secret societies, originating in the same selfishness, existed and flourished among the heathen; and, second, that not the most *trifling looking* toward evidence can be found that any sacred person mentioned in the Scriptures ever belonged to a secret society.

We admit and affirm that the essential elements of all secret societies existed in times which lie beyond the reach of reliable history, but they existed, we repeat, among the heathen, and in them we see the germinating principles and *prototypes* of all these associations. Though the modifications of selfishness are almost infinite, the essential features are immutably the same.

Masonry, however, justly claims considerable age. As to the precise time when it originated we have no very definite information, and are but little concerned to know. Masons, themselves, have endeavored, and with some success, to involve their origin in obscurity. This is an old device. The Romans were unwilling to acknowledge the humbleness of their origin, and therefore invented the fable that their city was founded by a son of Mars, one of the gods! The probability is that the following is a true account of the rise of this fraternity.

" Stone masons, in connection with ninety other trades and crafts, in the city of London, have been in the habit, for centuries, of meeting in clubs for the purpose of improvement in the elements of their business, and of architecture. Each craft has its public hall, its admission fee, its coat of arms, and its charity fund. The companies are given by name in the order of their rank in Ree's Cyclopedia, Art. " Company." And out of eighteen, whose form of government is particularly mentioned, sixteen are governed by a master, two wardens and a various number of assistants. So Freemason lodges are governed ; and the titles Worshipful, and Most Worshipful, now peculiar to Freemasonry, were common to gentlemen of the sixteenth and seventeenth centuries, as Esq. and Hon. are at the present day. The Lord Mayor of London at his election became a member of one of the twelve principal societies, (if he were not a member of one of them before), 'for these twelve,' says the Cyclopedia, 'are not only the oldest but the richest; many of them having had the honor of kings and princes to be their members; and the apartments of their halls being fit to entertain a monarch.' But Masons are not among the twelve first. Their rank is Hall No. 31, in Basinghall street; charter A. D. 1677, in the reign of Charles II."

From these humble but respectable mechanics, speculative Freemasonry, no doubt, arose. "Every symbol and article of clothing of the present day show this conclusively. Whence do they derive the origin of their aprons, trowels, plumblines, gavel, &c., if not from operative Masons? In the years 1716 and 1717 an attempt was successfully made to convert this system into speculative Freemasonry; and when at length many different trades were admitted, they raised it above its vulgar origin, and attempted to load it with pretensions of honor and antiquity. The records and constitutions were committed to the flames, that they might not give a lie to their assertions. The Mystic Circle or American Hand Book of Masonry substantially admits the correctness of the above view in the following: "During the reign of Queen Anne the annual festivals were entirely neglected, and the number of Masons considerably diminished. It was therefore determined that the privilege of Masonry should not be *confined to operative Masons*, but that persons of *all professions* should be permitted to participate in them, provided they were regularly approved and initiated into the order." p. 29.

" Three degrees only were then invented, and these were, in 1720, passed into the different nations having communication with Great Britain. At this time their historians are capable of giving the name of the Grand Master, the date of the warrant to a year, and the place where it was sent. Do they give the dates of warrants, or the operation of this society, previous to this? They are as silent as the grave, from the days of king Solomon down to 1717. Could they not have given the previous history with the same accuracy?" (*"Light on Masonry."*)

We believe the above to be an accurate history of the rise of, Freemasonry. However, as to the antiquity of Masonry we care very little. If it were of yesterday, or arose among the first products of the fall,—if it be as old as St. Paul's, of London, or the tower of Babel, it matters not. Its nature— its principles—are the same. A good institution is good, be it young or old; and a bad one should be discarded, be it ancient or modern. We believe Masonry is not as old as popery, though it is old enough to be honorable, if it be found in the way of righteousness.

The INDEPENDENT ODD FELLOWS seem to be making an effort to involve their origin in obscurity, and occasionally, in rather a bashful manner, they talk about having originated in the days of Julius Cæsar, who flourished some time before Christ! This is quite a respectable age—two thousand years! Where they have been all this time, what they have been about, and why no one knew anything about them until recently, no one, as I have heard, pretends to explain. In the absence of even a shadow of the most trifling evidence to the contrary, we shall be under the necessity of believing that this society is a production of late years—a recent modification of selfishness.

The SONS OF TEMPERANCE do not claim a high antiquity. They are in this, now, honest. Of the Rechabites, Rectifiers, Sons of Liberty, Daughters of Liberty, Red Men, Thousand and One, &c., &c., it is not important to speak. They are perhaps unworthy of notice. There is, however, a secret society existing in Hindostan, which ought not to be passed by without notice, as Christendom is indebted to Heathendom for secret societies. Caleb Wright, in his lectures on India, gives the following:

"The Hindoos, like the inhabitants of more civilized countries, have secret societies. The most remarkable of these is the society of the Thugs, which boasts of great antiquity. In some respects it is a religious society; for its members believe that they are under the immediate guidance and protection of Kali, and that she permits them to obtain their livelihood by murdering travelers on the highway, and then taking their property. It would be quite inconsistent with their religious principles to rob any person until he is first deprived of life by strangulation. They affirm that this system was first instituted by Kali, and is consequently of divine origin: that for many thousands of years she assisted them in escaping detection, by devouring the dead bodies of their victims; but, on a certain occasion, a Thug, contrary to her command, looked back to see how she disposed of the corpses, and saw her feasting on them. This circumstance so offended her that she declared she would no longer devour those whom they murdered. They believe, however, that she still continues to assist them, and that she directs their movements by certain omens."

The Thugs, who have flourished so exten-

sively in Hindostan, and deprived so many
innocent persons of their lives, by their secret
wickedness, will receive no further notice, as
they are not likely to be established in this
country.

II.

Arguments against all Secret Societies.

S we have seen from the preceding chapter, many secret societies have flourished and now exist in the world, some of which are of ancient origin, others claiming to be, and others still of recent invention. Of late, a wonderful revival in the regions of darkness, it seems, has taken place, and secret associations have come up all over the land, like the plague of frogs in Egypt. We have formed a slight acquaintance with the Rechabites, Rectifiers, Red Men, Sons of Liberty, A Thousand in One, Sons of Temperance, Odd Fellows and Freemasons. With the three last named we have had the largest acquaintance, and they are now the most influential. The Sons of Temperance, however, appear to have a very imperfect organization, and as a secret society could not, in our opinion, long exist. Provision, however, has been made to remedy this defect by the institution of the society of the "Temple of Honor"—an organization which the Sons are generally patronizing, and which *they* say, so far as I have conversed with them, is superior to their own order. They seem to regard it as a higher and more perfect order, having the advantage of the Sons in this, that the obligations are stronger, and there are a number of degrees, such as Masonry has, so that when a man is first admitted he is not at the end of the mystery, but may take another, and still another step in search of more light. The great ostensible object of the Temple of Honor is, I believe, temperance; but any man of discernment can see that the enemy having allayed the fears of many conscientious people by affirming that the "Sons" were not in reality a secret society, and thus inducing them to commit the temperance cause to their hands, is now making an effort to betray that sacred cause into the meshes of a secret society as objectionable and as dark as Masonry itself. Thus we have another example of the devices of

Satan. We shall regard the Sons and Temple of Honor as one in principle.

There are some arguments which lie with equal weight against all secret associations, and others which may be urged against a particular association. We shall now offer some of the first class:

I. *We are acquainted with no laudable object which cannot be accomplished more successfully without than with the aid of secret societies.*

If men wish to advance the temporal prosperity of the country, to dig canals, build railroads, put up lines of telegraph, improve harbors, establish mutual insurance, or promote any of the numerous interests of a neighborhood, state or nation, they do not form secret societies to accomplish those ends. What would we think of a secret railroad company? a secret mutual insurance company? or a secret society for the encouragement of agricultural pursuits? Or if men wish to advance the mental or intellectual interests of society, to promote general education, to encourage the fine arts to build up schools and colleges, they do not combine in secret conclaves for these purposes. Common sense would laugh at a "secret educational society," &c. And who would commit the unpardonable folly of creating a secret association for the promotion of the cause of religion? The Jesuits alone have done this, and that, not to establish the pure religion of Heaven, but the corruptions of Rome. All the interests of men—physical, intellectual, and religious—can be promoted successfully without the aid of secrecy, and the idea of attaching it to any of the societies which the real wants of the world demand, seems extremely unnecessary and even ridiculous.

The less of concealment, the greater the diffusion of all useful knowledge; the better people in general are acquainted with the useful and philanthropic operations of the day, the more useful they will become. Hence, all eminently useful societies have sought to let the public eye examine their origin, principles, manner of doing business, and, in fact, every thing about them.

The American Tract Society is accomplishing an extensive work in the world, but needs no concealment, no lodges guarded by a tyler, to shut out from the world its transactions, but invites the public to investigate everything about it with the greatest liberty. The public, therefore, have confidence in the society. They do not depend for their views of it upon the statements of its officers, but they can see for themselves. Were the chief meetings of that society in secret, and were the chief officers sworn under the most solemn obligations to conceal and never reveal what occurred in those meetings, who would say the public had not reason to suspect that society, and withdraw from it their support?

Christianity is more extensively and intimately connected with all the interests of human beings than any other system. And there is nothing, and can be nothing more important than its universal diffusion and reception. But the man who would propose to institute a society similar to Masonry or Odd Fellowship for the spread of pure Christianity, would be accounted wild. Nothing could be done with a secret society in the conversion of souls, and in training a community for Heaven.

And we may with propriety here inquire, if there is such a charm and power in secrecy in social organizations, why did not the Son of God, in some way, engraft it into Christianity? Or why did he not institute such a society to facilitate the reclamation of men? Or why did he not lay down some principle to give a warrant, expressly or impliedly, for such a society? Or, which is more to the point, why did he declare that he had resorted to no such means of doing good, but, on the contrary, SPAKE OPENLY, AND IN SECRET SAID NOTHING.

If, indeed, men propose to effect a good object by evil means, then, we admit, concealment is of much importance. Or if a society wishes to impose upon the world, and acquire a character which it does not *deserve*, then secrecy is almost indispensable. But when the objects are good, and the means proposed are good; when there is no dishonesty, double-facedness, or trickery, all may be done in open daylight, before the sun!

We repeat, this is the dictate of unsophisticated, unselfish common sense; and, as we have seen, it is the course pursued by all noble-minded men and combinations of men, whether they be united for the improvement of the country, the cultivation of the mind, or the spread of religion. From what has been said, may we not come to the following conclusions:

1. That every important object is, and may be, most successfully accomplished without the aid of secrecy or secret societies.

2. That secrecy would be a positive hindrance to any of the great philanthropic movements of the day, which are essential to the prosperity of the nation and church.

3. That, therefore, those societies which are secret—whose central and essential virtue is secrecy—are not suited to the wants of mankind, and cannot be extensively useful, if useful at all. And, as Christians, we are required to be good stewards, and not to waste the Lord's money, nor the golden hours he grants us; and as these cannot be usefully employed in secret societies, therefore a Chris-

tian is not justifiable in devoting either to
their use.

II. *Secrecy belongs legitimately to societies
which are combined for evil purposes.*

Corrupt and tyrannical governments, which
abuse the power conferred upon them by the
Universal Sovereign, usually proscribe liberty
of thought, of speech, and of the press, in
order to conceal from the public eye, as far
as possible, their odious and oppressive conduct.   Secrecy is almost, if not altogether,
essential to the success of tyranny; hence,
it will not suffer its acts and the people's
wrongs to be dragged into the light of public
scrutiny and investigation.   Thieves, counterfeiters, and other villains, who conspire
against society for the attainment of selfish
and devilish ends, have their associations,
and they are invariably secret associations.
They meet in lodges, under cover of the
night, with closed doors and windows, taking
every precaution to prevent the detection of
a single word or act.   They have their signs,
passwords, peculiar names, &c.   They are
sworn under the strongest penalties to be

true to their accomplices and let no secret escape them. Now every man can see the importance and even necessity of secrecy in such a combination. Divulgence would break it up and send all its members to the penitentiary or gallows. And we may remark that what is true of associated dishonesty is also true of dishonesty itself. Concealment is an essential element of its success, and perhaps the natural element of its being. The owl is frightened and unhappy when driven from his hollow tree into "noonday glory." But as we have already seen, it is no element of the success of societies confessedly good. On the contrary, Bible societies, tract societies, missionary societies and Sabbath school unions depend on being known, in a great degree, for success. These facts authorize us to conclude that secrecy is the legitimate badge and lawful property of corrupt and dishonest societies.

This conclusion may be deduced not only from the facts presented, but it is positively declared in the revelation of God:

"For every one that doeth evil hateth the light, neither cometh to the light lest his deeds should be reproved."

"But he that doeth truth cometh to the light, that his deeds may be made manifest that they are wrought in God."   John 3.

These are the words of Him who spake as never man spake, and they find a response in every Christian heart and rational mind. *Concealment* and *darkness* are interchangeable terms; and light signifies, in this connection, that which makes manifest and presents to unveiled observation.   The principle stated is this: Wicked deeds seek darkness, i. e., concealment, secrecy; while good deeds seek the light, i. e. observation; open, out-of-door, before-the-sun examination.   No skepticism can destroy this principle, no sophistry becloud it, no cunning undermine it.   It is as clear, and as solid, and as durable as the doctrine of Christ, and will stand while revelation stands and reason is sober.

We think the principle is clearly established, that secrecy is legitimately the badge or garment of dishonesty and villainy.   But we wish to be distinctly understood that we do not accuse all, nor a majority of the men who are connected with such organizations of dishonesty or corruption. By no means. Far be this from us. And before any man becomes offended, let him clearly understand our position. It is the *principle* we oppose, as wearing the face of dishonesty and villainy. And we leave it to the common sense of any man, if the assemblage of twenty men in a lodge, where every precaution is employed to prevent the discovery of a word that is spoken or an act performed, and where every man is sworn on his honor or his life staked, to conceal all that occurs from his dearest friend, has not a suspicious *appearance.* Does it not *look* like conspiracy? Has not such a meeting the badge which conspiracy wears? To say the very best of it, the *appearance* is evil; and we are commanded by an authority which we esteem paramount to all other authority, to "SHUN THE VERY APPEARANCE OF EVIL." We must, therefore, shun secret societies.

III. *Secret societies give to one class of men*

an advantage over other men, which an honest man and Christian does not want.

The truth of this proposition is evident, when we take into consideration the fact that the meetings of these societies are frequent, and that *the public have no means of ascertaining what they do.* They might resolve to cast their combined influence against one man and in favor of another, for reasons concerning which the former could know nothing. A snare might be secretly laid to entrap and ruin him, and he might be led into it by one under secret instructions, of which he would be, necessarily, entirely ignorant.

It may be replied, that any society or church might do the same, if they were so disposed. We reply, that any society or church might cast their combined influence against a man or set of men, but they could not do it *secretly.* They would have to do it *openly,* and the injured person would know from whence the influence came, and would be able to defend himself. That society would also be responsible to the public tribunal for its conduct. The difference is, a secret society can inflict an injury without committing itself before the public, or letting the injured know the fact. These are essential points of difference. And besides this, an open society cannot lay a plan or concoct a dishonorable scheme without letting the world know it; but a secret society may do all this.

And it would seem that for no other purpose can they be *secret* societies. As we have seen, there is no good object which can, in any way, be aided by secrecy, but it is a very important aid in many bad enterprises. Secrecy must be cherished for *some* object, and it is not insolent to ask for wha. object. Perhaps we may ascertain by supposing a case. If a society of Masons were confined alone upon an island, and were compelled to remain there during life, of what account would be their secrecy. All will answer, of no account whatever. And why of no account? Answer: Because there would be no uninitiated community surrounding. It is therefore clear, that the benefits or advantages of secrecy are to be derived, not from the secret society itself, but from the uninitiated. The design of secrecy is to give these societies certain advantages, which it would not be *proper* or *possible* to take *openly*.

But it may be asked, has this advantage ever been taken? We admit the power exists, and exists to be used, if needed; but can it be proven that any such sins have been committed? We answer, yes; such advantages have been taken. We have the testimony of quite a large number of seceding Masons, that such advantages are *frequently* taken. *Mr. Bernard*, an elder in the Baptist church, and a Mason of high rank, affirms that cases where such advantage of uninitiated persons is taken are not uncommon. *Avery Allyn* corroborates this testimony. Mr. Allyn gives an example of the application of this secret power in politics, in Connecticut, and affirms that such secret maneuvering is very common among Masons. The abduction and murder of William Morgan, and the successful resistance of the laws of New York by the masonic fraternity, affords an example in point, and a fact that needs no comment. But if it could be made to appear that this power to do evil had never been used, it would afford no apology for its existence, or reason for its encouragement. In a world full of depravity like ours, no such powers of destroying or undermining men should exist. What avails it that we live under a good government, if a secret inquisition may discuss our character; try us, if we provoke their resentment; and murder us, as William Morgan was murdered! How far this advantage may be used in church and state, or in matters of business, we cannot tell.

Many persons have been afraid to speak their sentiments, lest these orders should turn against them and injure them in their business or reputation. Now, every republican will say, that all good citizens should enjoy equal rights, and that no set of citizens should organize themselves into a society which gives them power, and bad men in that organization power, to take advantage of their fellow-citizens. And a Christian does not want any such power to take advantage. He discards and detests⸱ the villain's power to "strike, but conceal the hand." He believes where there is equality of virtue, there should be equality of privilege. He must, therefore, discard secret, oath-bound societies.

IV. *The plan proposed for the accomplishment of good, (and all these societies profess to be about that,) is unscriptural.*

This proposition will have no weight with an unbeliever, but with a Christian it ought to have great weight. A Christian is required to follow Christ, and derive from his precepts and spotless example, principles and rules of conduct. In all sincerity, and with the most scrupulous care, he should engage in no enterprise in which he may not have a conscience void of offence toward Christ, and upon which he may not ask, with a pure heart, the blessing of the Divine Saviour. "For whatsoever ye do in word or deed, do all in the name of the Lord Jesus."

This, to a man of weak faith and weaker piety, may appear over-much righteous; but to a Christian, Jesus is all and in all; and he would far prefer to live in banishment, alone with Christ, than to occupy the most exalted position in the gift of mortals, without him!

Now, there is not a passage in the whole Bible—not a sentence in the words of Christ, in particular—which gives the least encouragement, directly or indirectly, for the formation of a secret society. Show a " thus saith the Lord," in an express command, or an approved precedent for such societies, and we shall say no more. Where is the passage?— where is the authority? It cannot be found. On the contrary, Christ's plan of reform was directly opposite in character to the plan proposed by these societies. Hear his honest, daylight declaration, which no devotee of secrecy can use: "I SPAKE OPENLY AMONG YOU, AND IN SECRET HAVE I SAID NOTHING." To the Christian, Christ's plan of doing good is the best plan. He is a *model;* he alone is the master; and according to his rule the Christian is authorized, yea, it is his imperative duty, to work.

Masons say that their society existed in

the days of Christ's incarnation,—that John
the Baptist, and John the Evangelist, were
Masons.   Did Christ, then, belong to the Masons?   He who should affirm it, would be
accounted a fool or a maniac by Masons
themselves.   And if Jesus were now incar-
nate, does any one suppose that he would
enter the lodges of Masons or Odd Fellows?

No one dare affirm that he is following
Christ when he enters a lodge, and when he
is attired in all the gaudy regalia of these
orders.   The whole spirit of the religion of
Christ is plain, open, frank.   Heathenism, on
the contrary, has ever sought to shroud itself
in impenetrable mystery, and adorn its outside with spotted and showy garments.

The grand inviting principle of these
orders is secrecy.   Their motto is "To conceal and never reveal."   Their operations are
in the dark.   They work in the night.

The language of Christianity is, "Have no
fellowship with the unfruitful works of *darkness*, but rather reprove them."   The *principle*
upon which such associations are based is in
direct opposition to the genius of the Gospel;

hence the apostle immediately subjoins—"All things that are reproved are made manifest by the light, for whatsoever doth make manifest is light." The *doctrines* of the Gospel, we repeat, are proclaimed to the public ear, and court the examination of the most enlightened reason. The *designs* of the Christian institution are well known, and were proclaimed by its Author from Mount Olives —" Go teach all nations." The means to be employed are open to the inspection of all men, and, in a word, the whole of Christianity is *without concealment.*

Between Christianity and secret societies, therefore, there is a palpable contradiction of principle in the mode of doing good; and we honestly believe that conflict can never be compromised; that there never can be a peaceable union between the radiant light of pure Christianity and the labyrinthian darkness of such institutions. While the laws of God remain unchanged there can be no affinity between light and darkness, truth and error—or the open manliness of the Gospel and the skulking, behind-the-curtain, concealment plan of secret, oath-bound societies. We think it is clear: 1. That the secret agency plan of doing good is directly opposed in character to Christ's plan. 2. Christians are bound to follow Christ. 3. Therefore they must turn their backs upon all secret, oath-bound fraternities.

V. *Secret societies pretend to possess very valuable knowledge, which they are under the strongest promises and oaths to conceal from all the world, save members of their order.*

The Freemasons, especially, are frequently heard to speak in glowing terms of the "light," and "increasing light," which is poured upon the mind, at every degree. And all secret societies, to some extent, profess to possess within their lodges some charming knowledge, some almost unspeakable wisdom, too sacred for uninitiated eyes to gaze upon. There is a striking analogy, in this respect, between the secret societies of these days, and those "mysteries" of heathendom, which professed, anciently, to be the recipients and repositories of superlative wisdom. Everybody, without exception, now believes that the pretensions of those ancients were sheer hypocrisy.

We shall not now inquire whether these societies actually possess all this valuable fund of sacred wisdom; but shall suppose, for the present, that their high pretensions are just,—that they actually do possess a store of valuable knowledge, of which men in general are ignorant. What conclusion follows? Why, that these societies, in this concealment, are extremely selfish. Knowledge is the most valuable attainment—the richest inheritance—the real wealth.

> " Wisdom to silver we prefer;
> And gold is dross, compared to her."

Now, the testimony of the apostle James, and of common sense also, is, that a man is *selfish,* and cannot be a Christian, who hath an abundance of this world's goods, but refuses to impart of the same to the naked, shivering, hungry poor. How much more may we say, He that seeth his brother destitute of valuable knowledge, and refuses to impart of the abundance which he possesses, how dwelleth the love of God in him? In concealing this knowledge, he acts, or appears to act, the part of selfishness. He pretends to possess what would be valuable to his neighbors, but will not reveal it. No; not to father or mother, wife or brother,—not even to a most beloved disciple of Christ, can he, dare he, communicate a syllable.

The plain sense of men affirms that there ought to be a general diffusion of all useful knowledge. Who now looks with admiration upon those vain, self-inflated philosophers, who affected to be too wise to teach the multitude, and who pretended to monopolize a philosophy too pure and elevated for vulgar contemplation? and who does not entertain for Socrates a profound respect, because he labored to disseminate among the mass of the people the rich stores of knowledge he possessed?

Popes, tyrants, and secret societies, stand in singular unity against this verdict. There is nothing in the Gospel to warrant this selfishness; but, on the contrary, the disciples of Christ were required to communicate, as rapidly as possible, the precious truths committed to their trust. If, then, these societies do possess valuable knowledge, they are guilty of selfishness in concealing it from the world; if they do not, they are guilty of hypocrisy in their professions. But a Christian is neither *selfish* nor *hypocritical.*

The foregoing argument is based upon the assumption, that the profession of superior wisdom by secret fraternities is not hypocrisy. But we believe it is all mere pretence. Hundreds of Masons have declared that they were sadly disappointed, and that nothing of importance is learned in the lodge. And we may be permitted humbly to ask, Do the members of secret societies, with whom we are acquainted, manifest superior wisdom and prudence? Are they more sagacious in politics? are they better moralists —better theologians—better artists, mathematicians, linguists, astronomers, historians? No. As we have no *evidence* of superior wisdom, we conclude that the profession is all pretence. Yet the Masons, especially, speak continually of wisdom too sacred to be written! preserved by tradition!! Nonsense.

III

Arguments against all Secret Societies,

(CONTINUED.)

VI. *Secret societies establish a bond of union and brotherhood not recognized in the Scriptures, and which conflicts with and annuls the bond of union and communion established by God.*

"Well, what of it?" inquires the sneering skeptic. "Have not men a right to do as they please in forming associations?" Sure enough, what of it, if there is no truth in religion—if the Bible is a fable, and there is no Christ and no church of God? Just nothing at all. But I shall endeavor to show that there is much in this proposition which a *Christian* is under obligations to examine and weigh well.

The Scriptures *are* true, and from them we learn that God has established a bond of brotherhood and communion to which every other must give precedence. That union is in Christ. All, thus united, constitute the true and only church of Christ on earth. He is the head, they are the body. The apostle uses the human structure as an illustration of this grand idea. From the head of the natural body proceeds the clear thought, the sound understanding, the comprehensive judgment and vigorous will. So in Christ is found, in a certain sense, the intellect, the will, and the power of the church. There ought to be no schism in the church of Christ, which is his body.

As the rivulets issuing from the mountain side, join other rivulets in their descent, and thus united travel on in search of a common level and common union in the ocean, so do all Christians, in every clime, feel a power which draws and unites them together in the bosom of Christ. This is God's arrangement. This is the communion that God has established, and it is sacred.

But secret associations establish another bond of brotherhood, of which Christ is *not* head, and to unite in which it is not necessary to have faith in him, nor to know his regeneration. And the members of this brotherhood of secrecy are required to pledge their highest, strongest obligations of fidelity, and friendship, and love, to the members of this man-made fraternity, so that the duties of a Christian to a Christian are made to yield to the duties of a Mason, if you please, to a Mason. (I use the term *Mason* often when Odd Fellow or Templar would be equally applicable.)

I will state a strong case, which no Mason can deny and keep a good conscience. If a Mason who is an infidel, and a Christian brother who is not a Mason, are equally distressed, it is the duty of a masonic Christian to help, in preference, his masonic brother.

The Craftsman, a work issued by the Masons, in explaining the duties of Masons to their brethren, says, " Do good unto all," and then, as if to insult Christianity it adds: "more especially to the household of the faithful," page 22. Good Masons are here represented as belonging to, and *constituting*, the household of the faithful; and the scriptural injunction delivered by God to his people and church, is perverted and applied to an institution of men. Therefore, a Christian *Mason* is required to regard, not his brother in Christ, as a member of the household of the faithful, to whom he is *especially* bound to do good, but his brother in the secret lodge of which Christ is not head; and that brother in secrecy may be a Mormon, or Mohammedan, a universalist or an infidel. This mixed mass of unbelief and misbelief, joined in a bond of secrecy, is, according to the " *Craftsman*," the "household of the faithful!" " A cage," rather, " of unclean birds!"

Again, we quote on page 35: "To relieve the distressed is a duty incumbent on all men, but particularly on Masons, who are *linked together by an indissoluble chain of sincere affection*."

The Craftsman, in the above quotation, simply expresses what all the papers and books published by secret societies of every grade are continually affirming. The members of these fraternities regard each other as brothers in the highest sense of associated relation, and as bound to bestow upon each other especial regard, in preference to *all* others. When a man is initiated, he is constituted at once a brother worthy of being linked to all the members, whatever may be his moral state, in the chain of sincere affection. It is not pretended that initiation changes the heart or moral nature; consequently, this sincere affection arises as a result of law or rule.

Now we believe it is wrong for the Christian and infidel to be thus *linked* together. Christ contemplated the separation of his people from the world. "Ye are not of the world, but I have chosen you out of the world; therefore the world hateth you." "Whosoever, therefore, will be a friend of the world, is the enemy of God." "Be ye not unequally yoked together with unbelievers:" for what fellowship hath righteousness with unrighteousness? and what communion hath light with darkness? and what concord hath Christ with Belial? or what part hath he that believeth with an infidel?" Such is the law of Christ, pronounced by himself and his inspired Apostles. But secret societies unite in fraternal bonds men of all religions; or, in the language of the Craftsman, (which is an exponent, not only of Masonry, but of all secret societies on this point,) "*men of every country, sect and opinion.*" An effort is made to unite the believer and the infidel, the Jew and the Mohammedan, the Universalist and the Romanist, and, to complete the list, the wild Arab and the Mormon, in a chain, or, I would suggest, more properly, in a conglomerated mass of "sincere affection."

This position is stoutly denied by ignorant Masons and Odd Fellows. I am frequently told, that to be a good Mason or Odd Fellow it is required that a man believe in the existence of a God, so that a Mason or Odd Fellow who lives up to his creed is a *Christian.* Such ignorance is to be pitied rather than despised. These simple souls ought to know, that the bare acknowledgment that God exists, no more entitles a man to the character of a Christian, than the confession that the devil exists. Thomas Paine believed in the existence of a God, and wrote some passages of beautiful truth on his character. Mohammed believed that there was one God. All deists believe this much. Volney discoursed eloquently of the Supreme Architect of the Universe, and of morality. A deist, however, denies the inspiration of the Scriptures. He may say the Bible is a good book, that its morality is admirable, but that it is the *word of God* he denies. Again, the deist does not believe in Jesus Christ. He *may* believe that Christ was a good man, but he does not believe that he performed miracles, arose from the dead and ascended to heaven. He does not believe that he was the Son of God—that he was divine. A deist, in short, believes not the testimony which God has given of his son, and consequently makes God a liar!

We will now state three facts:—

1. A DEIST MAY BE A MASON, ODD FELLOW, OR SON.

2. A JEW MAY BE A MASON, ODD FELLOW, OR SON.

3. A MOHAMMEDAN MAY BE A MASON, OLD FELLOW, OR SON.

On the dedication of lodges belonging to

Masons we have the following: "But Masons *professing Christianity* dedicate theirs to St. John the Baptist, and to St. John the Evangelist, who were two eminent Christian patrons of Masonry." Some would infer from the above that Masons are somewhat religious, in dedicating their lodges to eminent Bible saints: but understand, this is said of those " who *profess Christianity*." As to those who do not profess Christianity, we are not told to whom they dedicate their lodges, but we may justly infer from the above remark, that Masons who are deists dedicate their lodges to whatever they please, that Mohammedans dedicate theirs to their prophet, and that the Mormons dedicate theirs to Gen. Joe Smith.

We quote again from the "Ancient Constitutions" of Masonry, Craftsman, p. 263: "But though in ancient times Masons were *charged* in every country to be of the religion of that country or nation, *whatever it was;* yet 'tis now thought more expedient only to oblige them to *that religion in which all men agree*, leaving their *particular opinions* to themselves."

From the above quotations, two facts are

evident: 1st, That Masonry in ancient times (if it existed then) patronized all religions—good, bad and indifferent—which is conclusive evidence that it then had no conscience. It authorized its adherents to worship at the feet of the "Grand Lama," at the car of Juggernaut, in a temple built to the sun, a mosque, a Jewish synagogue, or a Christian church. Such was the conscience of holy Freemasonry in its primitive purity.

But 2d, The same document informs us that of late the conscience of Masonry has become still more elastic, and it now only requires the observance of "*that religion in which all men agree.*" And please tell us what religion that is, in which all men agree? It is not Christianity, for that is everywhere spoken against. Strictly, there is no such religion. Deists, however, claim that their religion is one in which all men agree. "*There is one God.*" This is their creed. And as Masonry requires an acknowledgment of this creed and nothing more, it is justly inferable, that by the religion in which all men agree, the Ancient Constitutions mean deism. The naked acknowledgment that there is a God; which a Jew who scorns Jesus, an infidel who pronounces him an impostor, a Mormon, or even a devil, could make. The devil himself has religious belief enough to be a Mason. And we know that avowed deists have been elevated to, and now officiate in the office of "high priest" in Masonic lodges. And these examples are by no means uncommon.

But a deist, a Jew or Mohammedan may be an Odd Fellow. All the constitutions I have seen teach the religion of deism. There is before me the Constitution of the Columbia Lodge, No. 32. The article of faith reads as follows:—"To become a member of this lodge, the applicant must believe in the existence of a Supreme Being—Creator, Preserver and Governor of all things."

You will readily perceive that this confession can be made without a particle of faith in the Scriptures or in Christ.

In the Odd Fellows' Offering for 1844, we find the following: "Odd Fellows look abroad over the ample page of nature, and are satisfied with those gentle whisperings which tell of the divine from hill and dale, forest and mountain top." Here is a confession of faith! The Odd Fellow is "*satisfied*" with the "gentle whisperings" of nature—he does not feel the need of revelation.

Let us hear another Odd Fellow tell us what Odd Fellowship is: "What is Odd Fellowship? We answer in a word: it is practical Christianity. It combines all that is excellent in religion, pure in morals, and benevolent in practice. Beneath its sweet and gentle influences the rugged nature of man becomes softened by sympathy; the finer feelings of the heart are developed and cultivated; the social principle is strengthened; the fraternal relations cherished and invigorated. Before its onward progress wo and crime flee away; the unhappy fiends of unholy passion shrink into their dens of shame." (*The Talisman.*)

Such are the pretensions of a society into which an infidel, a blasphemer of Jesus Christ may enter, and does enter, and receive the highest honors! This society knows nothing of Jesus Christ, nothing of his atonement, nothing of faith, nothing of the church, and yet it claims to be "practical Christianity," as if its members could be *practical Christians* and *theoretical deists*. It rejects, or passes scornfully by every fundamental doctrine peculiar to Christianity, and yet pretends to combine *all* that is *excellent* in *religion*. Of course the whole doctrine relating to Christ is not considered excellent in religion, or, as Masonry has it, is *non-essential*. If therefore an Odd Fellow, whether he be a deist, Jew, or Mohammedan, is a practical Christian, and Odd Fellowship combines in it all that is excellent in religion, it is superior to any church (for we know of no church that can make *practical* Christians of theoretical deists,) and it is no wonder that many members of this fraternity boldly declare that their order *is* superior to, and does more good than any church.

These facts satisfy us that the RELIGION OF THESE SOCIETIES IS DEISTICAL. They profess a religion, but it is the cold and heartless religion of deism, borrowing something from, and in some degree conforming to, the prevailing religion. In Christendom they carry a Bible, in the land of Mohammedanism the Koran, in Heathendom the Shasters. They refuse to honor Christ, and yet talk about virtue— living virtuously, dying peacefully, and entering the lodge above. They studiously keep Jesus out of the lodge, in order that they may admit the hard-hearted deist who calls Him an impostor. This studied, subtle neglect, grieves a true Christian, and he can never consent to go where Christ is unwelcome, and where cold, dark infidelity, in which all men agree, is preferred to the pure doctrines which Christ brought to us in the travail of his soul, and sealed with his precious blood.

Having now established the purely worldly and really deistical character of secret fraternities, it cannot be doubted that a Christian is opposing Christ when he gives his influence to them; and that when he pledges his love and affection and is joined to them in the strongest ties, he is pledging his love to the enemies of Christ, and is becoming a helpmate to those who would crucify the Son of God afresh, and put him to an open shame.

When a Christian church unites with those societies, it becomes a friend to a specious infidelity, and thus gives its influence to principles which it is a part of its mission to destroy.

The continued importunity of these societies to the church is—" Do not be so strict, so bigoted ; there is no harm in our organizations; give us your influence, and you shall have ours." The boast of secrecy is, that she can unite believers and infidels, Turks and Christians, in indissoluble bonds, the very thing which God forbids—the very thing which the apostles so earnestly warned the church to avoid.

We repeat, secret societies endeavor to unite what God has not united—the church and the world. " The friendship of the world," such as they establish, " is emnity with God," so that he who would be a friend of the world, in the sense of uniting in deistical associations, " is the enemy of God."

" Come out from among them and be ye separate," saith God. " Nay," cries secrecy, "let us live in alliance ; let us join hands and work together as brethren, in friendship, love and fidelity. We will eat our own bread and wear our own apparel, only let us be called by thy name, to take away our reproach. Only let us borrow a kind of sacredness from our connection with religion to give us character." We protest against this, as an effort to encroach upon the church of Christ, to induce a compromise of its principles; and we regard a Christian who enters this worldly communion as recreant to Christ.

VII. *We object to the societies already named because they exclude women.*

It is true, the Sons of Temperance permit them to organize in a nominal connection with themselves, but that is all. They are not permitted to enter the same lodges or constitute one society.

Now it needs no uncommon sagacity to discover that no organization can ever become very efficient for good without the society and influence of women.

Savage nations do not appreciate the worth of woman's influence. They regard her as far inferior in intellect, and as occupying naturally a decidedly lower rank in the scale of being. Hence, in savage countries, they are slaves. As Christianity progresses, woman rises in influence, and a nation which is enlightened admits her into every important social organization, and brings her influence to bear as prominently as possible upon every good enterprise. The course pursued by secret organizations forms the only exception. They seem still to occupy the ground of uncivilized nations. They shut out from their enterprises the powerful and salutary influence of woman! In this there is an analogy between heathenism and secret associations, owing probably to the fact that the former gave birth to the latter. Women constitute half the human race, and physically, the weaker portion. The Masons profess to teach glorious truths and sublime mysteries; is it not important that women understand these truths and mysteries? The Odd Fellows, in common with all the rest, profess to teach, among many other excellent things, *purity*, *fidelity* and *love*. Is it not important that women understand these sublime virtues? The Sons of Temperance teach temperance, and plead that in the lodge influences are brought to bear which are calculated to fasten the principles of total abstinence upon the mind more firmly than can be done elsewhere. Now, should not women enjoy the benefit of these influences, and contribute to them? We are told they are not so likely to become intemperate as men are. We admit this, but it removes not the objection. If they are naturally more temperate than men, they could, if admitted to the society, cast a stronger influence in favor of the desired object. And as women are the mothers of men, it is all-important that they have all the ability that can be acquired in order to give to the minds of their children a healthful growth. If secret societies have no such aid to give, then our objection is removed. Many women, however, are intemperate; many thousands who move in high life are regular tipplers, privately, and they encourage the use of intoxicating drinks in the family and social circles. When not thoroughly imbued with the principles of temperance, who cannot see that their influence on the other side is great and dangerous. And so with the principles and objects of all moral or religious associations. If those principles are good, if those objects are commendable they need, and ought to have all the influence that can be brought to bear upon them. And no man who has been civilized and enlightened twenty-four hours can doubt the almost irresistible power of women in the social organization. What if women were excluded from our schools, from our churches, from our Bible, tract and Sabbath school organizations—could they prosper? Why, such exclusion would be conclusive evidence that we were only half-civilized, at most.

VIII. *Secret societies are selfish in their nature, and have a tendency to increase the selfishness of their adherents.*

These societies profess to have *light*, but they put it under a bushel, and refuse to let it shine out upon all. This is selfish. All their meetings, and they are frequent, have the resemblance, at least, of selfishness. They shut themselves up and suffer not a word to escape, and no one is permitted to participate in those assemblies. This looks so much like selfishness that we can give it no other name.

The benefits bestowed by them are indicative of the same spirit. Only the initiated are aided. The healthy, well-doing part of the community are bound together under the strongest obligations to promote each others' interests, and to aid each other. This is an enterprise dictated by the purest selfishness.

Selfishness, by which I mean a principle which seeks its own interest without regard to the interests of others, is the bane of human happiness, the very essence of sin itself. Men have, it is true, their own interests which it is their duty to attend to, but they are under obligations to attend to them in such a way as not to interfere with the interests of others. In a correct social state there are no covert acts, no cunning devices to overreach, but all transactions are open and understood. Companies in such a state may unite for specific objects, but the community know what those objects are, and what means are to be used in accomplishing them. But if a company secretly convene, week after week, it is concluded with reason that they have a selfish end in view, which would be defeated if the community in general knew what it was. Such an appearance these societies have. And the obligation the members of them take, to keep secret everything, to be faithful to their oaths, to keep exclusively the blessings of the order to themselves, has a tendency to foster that selfishness which grows spontaneously in the human heart, and which the holy, benevolent Redeemer seeks to crucify and eradicate from the soul.

IV

Oaths of Freemasonry.

WE entertain against Freemasonry special objections, on account of the oaths
which it administers to those who are admitted into the several degrees of the order.

The abuse, unlawful arrest, abduction and
murder of William Morgan, a few years
since, in our midst, aroused the public attention for a time, and was the means of bring-
ing to light the hidden wickedness and
depravity of this society. As Masonry and
all secret orders seem to be anxious to forget
those startling facts and developments, and
cause the community to forget them, we
think it will be proper to give a concise
statement of them, after which we will present the obligations which Masons take upon
themselves, and prove that the abduction
and murder of William Morgan was not a
violation of masonic obligations, but in accordance with them.

"On Sunday, of all the days in the week, the 10th of September, 1826, the coroner of the county of Ontario, State of New York, himself Master of the lodge at Canandaigua, applied to a masonic justice of the peace of that town for a warrant to apprehend William Morgan, living fifty miles off at Batavia. The offence upon which the application was based was larceny, and the alledged larceny consisted in the neglect of Morgan to return a shirt and cravat that had been borrowed by him in the previous month of May. Armed with this implement of justice, which assumes in this connection the semblance of a dagger, rather than of its ordinary attribute, a sword, the coroner immediately proceeded in a carriage, obtained at the public cost, to pick up, at different stations along the road of fifty miles, ten masonic brethren, including a constable, anxious and willing to share in avenging the insulted majesty of the law. At the tavern of James Ganson, six miles from Batavia, the same place which had been the head quarters of the night expedition against Miller's printing office, the party stopped for the night. Had that expedition proved successful, it is very probable this one would have been abandoned. As it was, the failure acted as a stimulus to its further prosecution. Early next morning five of the masonic beagles, headed by the masonic constable, having previously procured a necessary endorsement of their writ to give it effect in the county of Genesee, from a masonic justice of the peace, proceeded from Ganson's house to Batavia, where they succeeded in seizing and securing the man guilty of the alledged enormity, touching the borrowed shirt and cravat. A coach was again employed, the masonic party lost no time in securing their prey, and at about sunset of the same day with the arrest, that is, Monday, the 11th of September, they got back to Canandaigua. The prisoner was immediately taken before the justice who had issued the warrant, the futility of the complaint was established, and Morgan was forthwith discharged. It turned out that the person of whom the shirt and cravat had been originally borrowed, had never sought to instigate a prosecution for the offence. The idea originated in the mind of the masonic coroner himself. He had executed the plan of using the law to punish an offence of Masonry, to the extent to which it had now been carried. Morgan had been brought within the coil of the serpent, but he was not yet entirely at its mercy. Another abuse of legal forms yet remained to complete the operation. No sooner was the victim landed upon the pavement, exonerated from the charge of being a thief, than he found the same masonic Grand Master and coroner tapping him on the shoulder, armed with a writ for a debt of two dollars to a tavern-keeper of Canandaigua. Resistance was useless. Morgan had neither money nor credit, and for the want of them he was taken to the county jail. The common property and remedial process of the State was thus employed to subserve the vindictive purposes of a secret society.

"Twenty-four hours were suffered to pass, whilst the necessary arrangements were maturing to complete the remainder of the terrible drama. On the evening of the succeeding day, being the 12th of September, the same Grand Master coroner once more made his appearance at the prison. After some little negotiation, Morgan is once more released, by the payment of the debt for which he had been taken. But he is not free. No sooner is he treading the soil of freedom, and perchance dreaming of escaping from all these annoyances, than upon a given signal, a yellow carriage and grey horses are seen by the bright moonlight, rolling with extraordinary rapidity toward the jail. A few minutes pass, Morgan has been seized, and gagged, and bound, and thrown into the carriage, which is now seen well filled with men, rolling on as rapidly as before, but in a contrary direction. Morgan is now completely in the power of his enemies. The veil of law is now removed. All that remains to be done is to use the arm of flesh. Morgan is now taking his last look of the town of Canandaigua.

"It is a fact that this carriage moved along, night and day, over a hundred miles of well settled country, with fresh horses to draw it supplied at six different places, and with corresponding changes of men, to carry on the enterprise, and not the smallest let or impediment was experienced.

"With but a single exception, every individual concerned in it was a *Freemason*, bound by the secret tie; and the exception was immediately initiated by a unanimous vote of the Lodge at Lewiston. It afterward appeared in evidence that the Lodge at Buffalo had been called to deliberate upon it, and moreover that the Lodges at Le Roy, Bethany, Covington and Lockport, as well as the Chapter at Rochester, had all of them consulted upon it. There is no other way to account for the preparation made along the line of the road traveled by the party. Nowhere was there delay, or hesitation, or explanation, or discussion. Everything went on like clock-work, up to the hour of the evening of the 14th of September, when the prisoner was taken from the carriage at Fort Niagara, an unoccupied military post near the mouth of the river of that name, and lodged in the place originally designed for a powder magazine, when the position had been occupied by the troops of the United States. The jurisdiction was now changed from that of the state to that of the federal government, but the power that had the man was one and the same. It was Masonry that opened the gates of the Fort, by controlling the will of the brother, who for the time had it entrusted to his charge.

"On this same evening, there was appointed to take place, at the neighboring town of Lewiston, an installation of a Chapter misnamed Benevolent, at which the arch-conspirator was to be made Grand High Priest, and an opportunity was given to all associates from distant points to come together, and to consult upon what it was best to do next. Here it is, that in spite of the untiring labors of an investigating committee organized for the purpose, and in spite of the entire application of the force of the courts of the county to the eliciting of the truth, the details of the affair which thus far have been clearly exposed, begin to grow

dim and shadowy.   There is reason to believe
that Morgan was carried across the river in
a boat, at night, and placed at the disposal
of a Canadian Lodge at Newark.   The scru-
ples of one or two brethren, who hesitated at
the idea of murder, brought on a refusal to
assume the trust.   Consultations on this side
of the river followed, and messengers were
dispatched to Rochester for advice.   The final
determination was, that Morgan must die, to
pay the penalty of his violated oath.

"After this, everything attending the cat-
astrophe becomes more and more uncertain.
It is affirmed that eight Masons met and threw
into a hat as many lots, three of which only
were marked.   Each man then drew a lot,
and where it was not a marked lot he went
immediately home.   There is reason to believe that the three who remained, were the
persons who, on the night of the 19th or 20th
of September, took their victim from the fort
where he had been kept for sacrifice, carried
him in a boat to the middle of the stream,
and, having fastened upon him a heavy weight,
precipitated him into eternity!"   (See *Free-*

masonry, by J. Q. Adams, Encyclopedia Americana, Art. *Morgan.*)

Such is a statement of some of the leading facts connected with this case. From the day that it was known that Morgan was making arrangements with Miller to publish the secrets of the first three degrees of Masonry, the most untiring, dishonest, and wicked means were employed to destroy Morgan and Miller, especially the former. Anonymous letters of a slanderous and threatening character were circulated, and fire was set to Miller's printing establishment.

John Quincy Adams, who was an honest and careful observer of the facts connected with this case, enumerates the crimes committed by the Masons in the kidnapping and murder of William Morgan, in a letter dated Sept. 21, 1831. I will quote his own words:

" 1. Fraudulent abuse, in repeated forms, of the process of the law, to obtain upon false pretences possession of the person of Morgan.

" 2. Infamous slander in those false pretences, by first arresting him on a charge against him of petit larceny.

" 3. Previous slander in newspaper advertisements, denouncing him as a swindler and impostor, calling upon *brethren* and *companions* particularly to observe, mark and govern themselves accordingly, and declaring that the *fraternity* had amply provided against his evil designs.

" 4. Conspiracy of masonic lodges assembled in great numbers, *per fas et nefas*, by the commission of any crime to suppress this book.

" 5. Arson, by setting fire at night to Miller's printing office, in which were eight or ten persons asleep, whose lives were saved only by the early discovery of the projected conflagration.

" 6. Fraud, deception and treachery, in procuring from Morgan himself a part of his manuscript, which was finally sent by a special messenger to the General Grand Chapter of the United States, in session in New York.

" 7. Kidnapping, too successfully practiced upon Morgan—attempted upon Miller.

" 8. False imprisonment and transportation of Morgan beyond the bounds of the United States, into a foreign territory.

" 9. *Murder*—taking nine days in its preparation—keeping the wretched and helpless victim the whole of that time in a state of continual and cruel torture."

Mr. Morgan was torn from his wife and infant children by a false accusation, thrown into jail for an alleged debt of two dollars, though he offered his coat to pay it, discharged in the darkness of the night under pretence of friendship, and immediately seized by Masons, gagged to stifle his cries, put into a carriage and carried one hundred and thirty miles, lodged within the walls of an old fort, and there confined five days, denied the light of heaven, denied a Bible, denied the privilege of seeing his wife and children once more, and finally, in cold blood and after mature deliberation, plunged into the waters of the Niagara!

Now was all this in accordance with the obligations which Masons take upon themselves? We believe it was, and will adduce our evidence. These obligations were obtained by John Quincy Adams, from Col. W. L. Stone, a Mason and a Knight Templar. Col. Stone was an honorable man, and his veracity cannot be doubted.

The oath taken by an Entered Apprentice, which is the first degree, reads as follows:

"I, A. B., do, of my own free will and accord, in the presence of God, and of this right worshipful lodge, erected to God, and dedicated to holy St. John, hereby and hereon most solemnly and sincerely swear, that I will always hail, forever conceal and never reveal any of the secret or secrets of Masons or Masonry, which at this time, or any time hereafter shall be communicated to me as such, except it be to a true and lawful brother, or within the body of a just and regular lodge, him or them whom I thus find to be, after strict trial and due examination.

"I furthermore promise and swear, that I will not write them, stamp them, stain them, cut them, carve them, mark them, work or engrave them, nor cause them so to be done, upon anything movable or immovable under the canopy of Heaven, capable of bearing the least visible sign, mark, character or letter, whereby the mysteries of Masonry may be illegally obtained.

"All this I do solemnly swear, with a full and hearty resolution to perform the same, without any evasion, equivocation, or mental reservation, under no less penalty than to have my throat cut across from ear to ear, my tongue plucked out by the roots, and buried in the rough sands· of the sea, a cable's length from the shore, where the tide ebbs and flows twice in twenty-four hours. So help me God, and keep me steadfast in this my obligation of an Entered Apprentice."

Fellow Craft's Obligation.—In the next degree of Masonry above named, the obligations and the penalties increase. We will quote the penalty annexed to a revelation of any of the secrets of Masonry in this degree:

"All this I solemnly and sincerely swear, with a full and hearty resolution to perform the same, without any evasion, equivocation or mental reservation, under no less a penalty than to have my heart taken from my left

breast, and carried to the valley of Jehosha-
phat, there to be thrown into the fields, to
become a prey to the wolves of the desert,
and the vultures of the air."

A Master Mason's Obligation.—Among the
things promised in the obligations of this
degree the following is found :

" I furthermore promise that I will attend
a brother barefoot, if necessity requires, to
warn him of approaching danger,   *   *   *
that I will keep his secrets as safely deposited in my breast as they are in his own,
treason and murder only excepted, and those
at my option."

All this is done with " no less a penalty
(upon forfeiture) than to have my body cut
across, my bowels taken out and burnt to
ashes, and those ashes scattered to the four
winds of heaven; to have my body dissected
into four equal parts, and those parts hung on
the cardinal points of the compass, there to
hang and remain as a terror to all those who
shall presume to violate the sacred obligation
of a Master Mason."

In the Craftsman, it is declared that the

secrets of Masonry are preserved under the *"strongest penalties."* It appears that these penalties are such as above described. Masons have endeavored to explain away the barbarity of these oaths by calling it simply an imprecation, as if the swearer should say, "may I have my throat cut from ear to ear," &c. On this evasion, John Quincy Adams remarks: "Some of the masonic defences alledge that it is only an imprecation! "Under no less a penalty than to have my throat cut" . . . . a mere imprecation? Is it not then paltering with words in a double sense? A *penalty* is not an *imprecation;* and to have the throat cut across and the tongue torn out by the roots, is not expulsion from a lodge. The substance of the defence is, that the penalty is a *brutum fulmen*; that there is no authority existing in, or conferred by the institution to carry it into execution; and that it is a special charge to all Masons upon their admission, to observe faithfully the laws of God and of the land. But for every degree of Masonry there is a separate oath, and a diversified penalty, and in some of the higher degrees it includes a promise to carry into effect the punishments of the fraternity. I have heard of the instructions from the owner of a piratical cruiser to his captain, directing him to take, burn, sink or destroy, any merchant vessel of any nation that might fall in his way, and to dispose of the people on board of them so as that they might not prove afterwards troublesome; but to be especially careful not to infringe upon the laws of nations or of humanity. This man must have been a Mason of at least the Royal Arch degree."

We conclude from the reading of these three oaths, (and Morgan had taken them,) that the murder of William Morgan was in strict accordance with masonic law and principle. As says the writer above quoted: "The oath, the penalty, the secret, and Morgan's corpse at the bottom of Niagara river, where a shrewd brother of the craft 'guessed he would write no more books,' are illustrations of each other, which it would take much sophistry to obscure:, much prevarication to confuse."

Mr. Allyn, who was a Knight Templar, made oath before a magistrate in the city of New York, that it was so communicated to him in an encampment of Knights Templars, in St. John's Hall, New York, March 10th, 1828, that Morgan had been murdered. Much effort, of course, has been made to discredit Allyn's testimony, but Col. Stone, in his letters on *Masonry and Anti-masonry*, page 238, frankly acknowledges that "having long disbelieved the statement, he did finally satisfy himself that it was substantially true." And this Col. Stone, be it remembered, was himself a Knight Templar.

That these are the obligations assumed by Masons, cannot with any degree of plausibility be denied. They are declared to be such by *David Bernard*, a respectable minister in the Baptist church, who was also a Mason of high degree. I will here insert, for the reader's benefit, Elder Bernard's own language in regard to his connection with masonry, and his knowledge of its character and obligations. He speaks like a candid man:

"Soon after I commenced the service of Christ, Freemasonry was presented to me as an institution from heaven; moral, benevolent, of great antiquity, the twin sister of Christianity, possessing the patronage of the wise, the great, the good; and highly important to the ministers of the Lord Jesus. Wishing to avail myself of every auxiliary in promoting the glory of God and the happiness of my fellow-men, I readily received the three first degrees. My disappointment none can know but those who have in similar circumstances been led in the same path of folly and sin. I silently retired from the institution, and for three years was hardly known as a Mason. I was not, however, without my reflections on the subject. I considered what I had taken as frivolous and wicked; but was unwilling to believe that there was no substantial good in the order; and this idea was strengthened from the fact that many of my friends of a higher grade in masonry taught me that what I had received was not the *magnum bonum* of the institution, but that this was yet to be at-

tained.   Not being able to advocate its cause
from the knowledge I had derived from its
principles, and supposing that the obligations
I had received were morally binding, I could
not say *pro* or *con* concerning it, without
a violation of my conscience.   With these
views I embraced an offer to advance into the
higher orders of mysticism, and reached forward to attain the desired end.

"In the reception of the chaptoral degrees,
my embarrassment increased. When I came
to the oath of a Royal Arch Mason, which ob-
ligates to deliver a companion, 'right or wrong,'
I made a full stop and objected to proceeding.
I was then assured in the most positive terms,
that all in the end would be explained to my
full satisfaction.   But no such explanation
took place.   Thought I, is this Freemasonry?
Is this the ancient and honorable institution
patronized by thousands of the great and
good?   Upon my suggesting some queries
to a masonic friend, he gravely informed me
that the first seven degrees were founded on
the Old Testament, and were but a shadow
of good things to come; that if I wished to

arrive at *perfection*, I must proceed to the sublime and ineffable degrees. The assurances,
the awful oaths I had taken, with the penalties and the vengeance of this most powerful
institution, combined to deter me from re-
nouncing it as an evil. After much deliberation, hoping to find something in the higher
orders to redeem the character of the institution in my estimation, I entered the lodge
of perfection and took the ineffable degrees.

"About this time I learned that William
Morgan was writing masonry for publication.
My informer was then a Baptist minister in
high standing, and a Royal Arch Mason. He
remarked that Morgan's writing Masonry was
the greatest piece of depravity he ever knew;
that some measures must be taken to stop it;
that he would be one of a number to put him
out of the way; that God looked upon the institution with so much complacency, he would
never bring the perpetrators to light; that
there had already been two meetings on the
subject, and that he expected there would be
another on that day, and finally attempted

to justify his murder, from Masonry and the Word of God!

" This conversation took place in Covington, (where I then lived,) five weeks before Morgan was murdered; and I should at this early period have informed him of his danger, had I not understood that he was on his guard, and prepared for defense.

" The next week I left home for my health, and was absent some weeks. I returned on the 16th of September, and soon learned that Morgan was murdered! I conversed with Masons on the subject, and *they justified both his abduction and murder!* I now read the production of Elder Stearns on Masonry with peculiar interest. I also examined the Monitor, and other masonic writings, and reflected deeply on the nature and tendency of the institution. I compared the murder of Morgan and the conduct of the fraternity in relation to his abduction, with the oaths and principles of the order, and became fully satisfied that to continue longer with the institution was not my duty.

" I expressed my opposition to its principles,

and the recent conduct of the fraternity, in a free and open manner, which caused much excitement among the brotherhood. A meeting of the lodge in Covington was soon called, the object of which was to concert measures for an agreement among the fraternity, in what they should say in relation to their outrages, and to attend to members who were disaffected with their proceedings. I attended for the purpose of freeing my mind. When the lodge was duly opened, and the subject introduced, I arose, and in the most decisive manner disapproved the conduct of the fraternity, in their violation of civil and moral law. The meeting was long and *horribly* interesting! The true spirit of the institution was manifested, especially toward me. For the introduction of Elder Stearns' book, and the honest expression of my sentiments, I was most shamefully abused. THE MURDER OF MORGAN WAS JUSTIFIED, and everything said that was calculated to harrow up the feelings of a patriot or a Christian. Elder A****, a Knight Templar, being present, boldly asserted, that if he should see any man writing masonry, *he should consider it his duty to take measures to stop him;* that as cities and churches had their laws, with a right to inflict their penalties, so Masons had their laws, with the right to inflict the penalties to them; and that the lodge was the place to try a Mason;—that if Morgan had been writing masonry, and his throat was cut from ear to ear, his tongue torn out by the roots, and his body buried beneath the rough sands of the sea, at low water mark, where the tide ebbs and flows twice in twenty-four hours, he could not complain of not having justice done him! 'Amen! Amen! Amen!' was the audible response around the room."

In the above we have the testimony of a man whose word can never be disputed by those who are disposed to be reasonable, concerning the obligations of masonry in their connection with the abduction and murder of Morgan. Beside the testimony of Elder Bernard, we have the witness of a convention of seceding Masons, who met at Le Roy, Feb. 19th, 1827. Beside this, another convention of Masons, assembled at Le Roy, N. Y., July

4th, 1828, bore witness to the same melancholy facts.

If we are disposed to be influenced by the most unimpeachable testimony, we shall be driven to the conclusion that the Masons did not violate their masonic oaths when they murdered William Morgan.

V.

The Obligations of Masonry.

WE think it will be useful and highly
interesting to present here, in conclusion of this subject, an entire letter, written
by one of the strongest minded men whom
America has ever produced—JOHN QUINCY
ADAMS. He interested himself much, during
a period of his life, on the subject of Masonry. He examined carefully the Morgan
affair—the concessions, confessions and various publications of seceding Masons, and
the defenses published by the Order. No
one will say that Adams was not *honest*. Nor
will any one say he lacked discernment, or
that he was a superficial observer. He wrote
a large number of letters to different persons
on the subject of Freemasonry. A number
were directed to Edward Livingston, Esq.,
who was the General Grand High Priest of

the order in the United States.   These letters
were written on masonic oaths, and were
designed to prove that the murder of Morgan
was in accordance with those oaths, and not
in violation of them.   We present one letter
entire, extracted from a volume of his letters
recently published.

To Edward Livingston, Esq.

QUINCY, 1st May, 1833.

SIR—The Entered Apprentice's oath, obligation and penalty, upon which I undertook
to animadvert in the four letters to Col. Wm.
L. Stone, a copy of which was transmitted
to you, with the first of these letters to yourself, was in the terms of that obligation as
furnished by the officers of the Grand Lodge
of Rhode Island themselves, to the committee
of the Legislature of the State, appointed to
investigate the charges against the institution which had been made since the murder
of Morgan, and which they and you pronounce calumnious.   The obligations themselves had never been authenticated by the

authority of adhering Masons, until they
were produced by the officers of the Grand
Lodge and Grand Chapter, at the peremp-
tory requisition of the legislative committee.
They were generally considered by Masons
as constituting essential parts of the mysteries of the craft, and included strictly within
the promise never to write, print, cut, carve,
paint, stain, or engrave them. In the practice of the chapters and lodges, the oaths
are all administered by rote, and pass by
tradition alone. This is of course the cause
of the differences in the phraseology of the
oaths as administered by different persons.
It is one of the great inherent vices of the
institution. It affords constant opportunity
and frequent temptation to every chapter
and lodge to make additions to the promises
pledged by the recipient of each degree.

The manuscript obligations furnished by
the Grand Chapter and Grand Lodge of
Rhode Island were drawn up and reduced to
writing for the occasion. The Grand Lodge
had previously published a defense of Masonry, stoutly denying that there was anything

in the Masonic obligations contrary to religion, morals, or laws of the land; but carefully abstaining from any statement of what they were.   They had used that notable device of explaining the penalty of death *for* revealing the secrets of the craft, or of any of its members, as meaning only a promise to suffer death *rather* than reveal them.   They had expounded, and explained, and denied the several parts and parcels of the Masonic obligations, till they had made them all as innocent as their lambskin aprons.   They had especially denied, with abundance of indignation, that they had ever administered or taken the oath to conceal the secrets of a brother mason—" murder and treason not excepted."   These words, or others equivalent to them, are stated in Elder Bernard's Light on Masonry, and in Avery Allyn's Ritual, to form a part of the Royal Arch obligation. They are certified as such by the convention of seceding Masons, held at Le Roy on the 4th of July, 1828, twenty-three of whom had taken this oath; and they have since been attested by adhering Masons, upon trials before judicial tribunals in the State of New York. They are not in the Royal Arch obligation, reported by the Grand Chapter of Rhode Island; but in the Master Masons' obligation, reported by the Grand Lodge. Among the promises of admission to that degree are the following words: " That I will keep a brother's secrets as my own, when committed to me in charge as such, murder and treason excepted." This, of course, is a pledge of immunity for all other crimes; but it does except murder and treason. So said the Grand Lodge of Rhode Island. Yet even in that state, Nathan Whiting, an attorney and counsellor at law, who had taken the degree in the lodge at East Greenwich, and had been Master of that lodge, testified that in the Master's degree, after " murder and treason excepted," the usual form was to add, " AND THAT AT MY OPTION ;" and what the difference is between that and " murder and treason *not* excepted," I leave as a problem in morals for masonic casuists to solve.

In the seventh of Col. Stone's Letters upon Masonry, page 66, referring to the disagreement in the phraseology of the obligations, as given in' different places, he makes mention of a manuscript then in his possession, containing copies of the obligations of the several degrees, as they were given twenty-three years before in the lodge and chapter of an eastern city—copied from the manuscript of a distinguished gentleman, who had been Master of the lodge and High Priest of the chapter. The forms, says Col. Stone, are the same that were used in that city for a long series of years; and when Royal Arch Masonry was introduced *into Rochester, in the State of New York, these forms, from these identical papers, were then and there introduced and adopted.*

There is at this passage a reference to a note in the appendix, stating it to have been the original intention of Col. Stone to insert all the obligations contained in that manuscript in his text; but he was compelled to suppress them from the unforeseen extent of his work. He observes that neither of the obligations in the first three degrees, in those manuscripts, is more than half as long as those disclosed by Morgan, and in common use. He further adds that these manuscripts give a more sensible, and intelligible, and a less exceptionable account of the seven degrees of Masonry than any other work he had seen; and he concludes by observing that *when Morgan was at Rochester these papers were there, and already written to his hands.* It is to be regretted that Col. Stone did not adhere to his first intention of publishing these obligations, or rather that he did not insert the whole manuscript in his appendix. I have obtained it from him, and annex hereto the three obligations, as there recorded, of the Entered Apprentice, the Fellow Craft, and the Master Mason. [These will be found in the preceding chapter of this work.—ED.] It will be found, upon examination, that although truly represented by him as perhaps not half so long as the same obligations in Morgan's and Bernard's books, they lose nothing of pith and moment by the retrenchment of words. They were the forms used at Rochester, and no other masonic institution in the State was more

deeply implicated in the tragedy of the kidnapping and murder of Morgan than that
same chapter at Rochester.   Now, in the
Entered Apprentice's oath of that manuscript, the promise is expressly and explicitly
to keep and conceal the secrets of Masons as
well as Masonry.   The penalty is the same
as that reported by the Grand Lodge of
Rhode Island, but in the lecture to the candidate on his admission, there is in the manuscript an *explanation* of the meaning of the
penalty, which not only utterly falsifies the
explanation of the Rhode Island Masons, so
strangely accepted and countenanced by the
majority report of the legislative investigating committee, but proves that the MURDER-
ERS OF MORGAN understood but too well the
real character of the obligation.

In this Entered Apprentice's Lecture, the
candidate, after going through the forms of
admission, is examined by the Master, upon
interrogatories with regard to the meaning
of all the ceremonies through which he has
passed.

Upon giving the account of his admission at the door, the following, word for word, are the questions put to him by the Master, and his answers:

" *Q.* What did you next hear?"

" *A.* One from within, saying with an audible voice, let him enter."

" *Q.* How did you enter?"

" *A.* Upon the point of a sword, spear, or other warlike instrument, presented to my naked left breast, accompanied by this expression—do you feel?"

" *Q.* Your answer?"

" *A.* I do."

" *Q.* What was next said?"

" *A.* Let this be a prick to your conscience, a shield to your faith, AND INSTANT DEATH IN CASE YOU REVOLT."

Yes sir, this is the explanation given to the Entered Apprentice, at the time of his admission to the degrees, of the penalty under which he binds himself by his oath. This was the formula in *Connecticut* more than twenty-five years since, and thence introduced into Rochester, in the State of New York. Who shall say that the murderers of Morgan misunderstood the import of the Entered Apprentice's obligation?

And in this same manuscript of the forms of admission used at Rochester, the following, word for word, are clauses of the Master Mason's obligation:

"I furthermore promise and swear, that I will attend a brother barefoot, if necessity requires, to warn him of approaching danger; that on my knees I will remember him in my prayers; that I will take him by the right hand and support him with the left, in all his just and lawful undertakings; that I will keep his secrets as safely deposited in my breast as they are in his own, *murder and treason only excepted*, AND THOSE AT MY OPTION; that I will obey all true signs, tokens, and summonses, sent me by the hand of a Master Mason, or from the door of a just and regular Master Mason's lodge, if within the length of my cable-tow."

This was the form of admission to a Master Mason's degree, when the chapter at Rochester decided that Morgan had incurred the penalties of his obligations, and sent out their signs, tokens and summonses, accordingly. These were the oaths which every Master Mason admitted at the lodge in Rochester had taken. All this he had most solemnly and sincerely promised and sworn, with a full and hearty resolution to perform the same without any evasion, equivocation, or mental reservation, under no less penalty than to have his body cut across, his bowels taken out and burned to ashes, and those ashes scattered to the four winds of heaven; to have his body dissected into four equal parts, and those parts hung on the cardinal points of the compass, there to hang and remain as a terror to all those who shall presume to violate the sacred obligation of a Master Mason.

Col. Stone, in his seventh letter, page 67, says, that in his apprehension the words *"and they left to my election"* are an innovation, and that he has not been accustomed to hear the obligation so conferred. The words in his own manuscript are, "and those at my option;" fewer words, but bearing the same meaning. They were no innovation at Rochester.

The only words in this obligation which need any explanation, are the words *cable-tow ;* and they are always so explained as to give them a definite meaning.   The rest are all as explicit as language can make them, and they are taken with a broad and total disclaimer of all evasion, equivocation or mental reservation.   So they were taken at Rochester, and so they are recorded in the old manuscript of Col. Stone.

You are a classical scholar, sir, and you doubtless remember the humorous remark of Cicero, in his dialogue on the nature of the gods; that he could not conceive how one Roman Haruspex could look another in the face without laughing.   I find it equally difficult to conceive how you, performing the functions of a Master of a lodge, as among the duties of a Grand High Priest you may be required to do—how you can look into the face of a man after administering to him such an oath as this, without shuddering. But we have not done yet with the old manuscript of Col. Stone.

After the ceremonies of admission to the

degree of Master Mason are completed and
the recipient has been invested in his new
dignity, he is conducted to the Master of the
Lodge in the East, there to hear from him
the history of the degree. There, sir, with
equal regard for historical truth, and reverence for the Holy Scriptures, you mingle up
the building of Solomon's temple, as recorded in the Bible, with the murder of
Hiram Abiff, by three Tyrian Fellow Craft,
Jubela, Jubelo, and Jubelum, as preserved in
the chronicles of masonic mystery. You
relate them all as solemn truths of equal
authenticity, and in the manuscript now
before me, the story goes that after the murder of Hiram Abiff was consummated, King
Solomon was informed of the conspiracy,
and ordered the roll to be called, when the
three ruffians were missing. Search was made
for them, and they were found by their dolo-
rous moans in a cave. Oh, said Jubela, that
my throat had been cut across, [&c., repeating the whole penalty of the Entered Apprentice's obligation,] before I had been
accessory to the death of so good a Master.

Oh, said Jubelo, that my heart had been torn out, [&c., repeating the whole penalty of the Fellow Craft's obligation,] before I had been accessory to the death of our Master. Oh, said Jubelum, that my body were cut across, my bowels taken out and burnt to ashes, [&c., repeating the whole penalty of the Master Mason's obligation,] before I had been the death of our Master, Hiram Abiff. They were then taken and sent to Hiram, King of Tyre, who executed on them the several sentences they had invoked on themselves, WHICH HAVE EVER SINCE REMAINED THE STANDING PENALTIES IN THE THREE FIRST DEGREES OF MASONRY.

This, sir, is the history of the Master Mason's degree, which was delivered by the Master of the Lodge at Rochester to every individual received as a Master Mason. This was the explanation given to him of the obligation assumed by him, immediately after the administration of the oath. This is, in substance, the explanation which you * * * * must give to every Master Mason whom you receive, of the penalty of the oath

which you administer to him in the name of
the everliving God—without evasion—without equivocation—without mental reservation.

And will you say, sir, as the Grand Lodge
of Rhode Island have said, that these penalties mean no more than that the swearer who
invokes them upon himself will *rather* die
like Hiram Abiff, than reveal the secrets of
Masonry? Is it Hiram Abiff in this story
who pays the penalties of violated vows?
Is it Hiram Abiff who invokes these penalties upon himself? The Entered Apprentice,
the Fellow Craft, and the Master Mason
invoke upon themselves the penalties of
their respective degrees. The Entered Apprentice is told that he enters the Lodge
on the point of a naked sword, pricking his
left breast, to remind him of INSTANT DEATH
IN CASE OF REVOLT; and the Master Mason is
told that the penalties executed upon Jubela,
Jubelo, and Jubelum, have ever since remained *the standing penalties in the three first
degrees of Masonry.*

And now, sir, what are we to think of
High Priests, and Royal Arch Chapters, and

Grand Masters, and Grand Lodges, who, after taking and administering in secret these oaths, with these penalties, for a long series of years, when their real character has been proclaimed by the voice of *midnight murder* from the waters of Niagara, in tones to which the thunders of her cataract are as a whisper —when their unequivocal import has been divulged, to the amazement, and disgust, and horror of all pure, unsophisticated minds; what are we to think of High Priests, and Grand Kings, and most illustrious Knights of the Cross, who face it out, in defiance of the common sense and common feeling of mankind, that there is nothing in these oaths and penalties inconsistent with the duties of those who take and administer them, to their country or their God? The manuscript from which I now give to the world the three obligations of the Entered Apprentice, of the Fellow Craft, and of the Master Mason, is, upon the testimony of Col. Stone, a Knight Templar and a man of unimpeached integrity, *Masonry in its most mitigated and least exceptionable form.* It was the Masonry of Connecticut more than twenty-five years since, and for many years before;—it was the Masonry of Rochester at the time of the murder of Morgan.

I have yet more to say to you, sir, on this subject, nor shall I be discouraged from continuing to address you, by your observance of a "dignified silence." If my letters are not read by you, there are those by whom they will be read, I trust, not without effect. If the presses under your jurisdiction, masonic or political, refuse their columns to the discussion of masonic morals, when the Grand High Priest is Secretary of State of the Union, it may serve to illustrate the subserviency of the periodical press to Masonry. But your address to your companions and brethren, at your installation as the Grand High Priest of the Royal Arch of this Union, is not the perishable effusion of a day. It is a state paper for history and biography—for the present age and for the next. It shall not be lost to posterity; it shall stand as a beacon to future time—the admiration, or at least the wonder of other generations.

JOHN QUINCY ADAMS.

VI.

Miscellaneous Objections to Masonry

E shall now adduce some miscellaneous objections to Masonry in particular, which ought to have considerable weight on the general subject. If it be thought that we devote too large a proportional space to this institution, let it be remembered that Masonry is the PATTERN by which all other secret combinations in this country have been constructed, and very many of the objectionable features found here have been copied into them.

1. *We object, because secrecy is regarded as an indispensable and essential virtue.* We quote from the Craftsman, page 216, the following singular morality: " The virtue indispensably requisite in Masons is secrecy. This is the guard of their confidence, and the security of their trust. So great stress is to be laid upon it, that it is enforced under the strongest penalties and obligations."

Secrecy is the guard of their confidence, and so great stress is laid upon it that it is enforced under the *strongest penalties;* and we have seen in a former chapter what those penalties are.

This is indeed a singular *virtue,* and one that is not enumerated among the virtues of any other societies which profess to be engaged in well-doing; but it *is* regarded as an essential *vice* in various societies which have evil objects in view.

It is a little singular that those good old saints, of whom Masons are ever speaking as patrons of their order, did not say something in their writings of this virtue. There is Solomon, and the two Johns, who recommend all the virtues requisite to qualify a man for heaven; but say not one word of this essential virtue of Masonry. And the other sacred writers appear to have presented a very defective practical theology; for not one of them ever hints that secrecy is a prominent virtue, or a virtue at all.

Christians are commanded to add to their faith virtue, and to virtue knowledge, and to

knowledge temperance, and to temperance—
secrecy ?—no, it is not found in all the cata-
logue of Bible virtues.   The Bible knows no
such virtue—it is entirely alien to Christianity.   Heathenism knew such a virtue—in
heathendom it became immensely popular, a
leading virtue—and out of heathenism it
originated, as will be seen by reference to
the first chapter of this book.   Let any
Christian show where this pretended virtue
is recommended in the Bible under the
strongest penalties, or where it is even recommended at all.   We can show on the
contrary that the principle on which it is
founded is wrong and *un*scriptural.

"No man, when he hath lighted a candle,
putteth it under a bushel, but on a candle-
stick, and it giveth light unto all that are in
the house.   Let your light so shine before
men," &c.   If the Saviour had said, "Light
your candle and put it under a bushel," then
we should have one passage of scriptural
authority for this pretended, and to all secret
societies, *essential* virtue.   We object—

2. *To the reasons assigned for other virtues.*

The following is the reason offered for *temperance*: "This virtue should be the constant practice of a Mason, as he is thereby taught to avoid excess, or contracting any wicked or vicious habits, the indulgence of which might lead him to "—[ruin his soul or dishonor God? no! but to] "disclose some of those valuable secrets which he has promised to conceal and never reveal." Here it is: a Mason should be temperate lest he reveal some valuable secrets while drunk! Wonder how many valuable things a drunken man could communicate to this dark age!

Fortitude is also enjoined as a leading virtue, and, in the language of the Craftsman, should be deeply impressed upon the mind of every Mason, as a safeguard against any illegal attack that may be made by force or otherwise, to extort from him any of those valuable secrets with which he has been so solemnly trusted. Masons are here exorted to cultivate fortitude, not that they may be able to resist temptations to sin, and perform the civil and religious duties incumbent upon Christians, but that they may preserve the valuable secrets intrusted to them so solemnly.

Prudence—"should be particularly attended to in all strange or mixed companies, never to let fall the least sign, token, or word, whereby the secrets of Masonry might be unlawfully obtained."

Behold now, if you wish to see an illustration of the sublimely ridiculous in morals, three cardinal virtues solemnly enjoined for the especial support of secrecy—which is a virtue only in the vocabulary of secret societies, but in reality a vice.

3. *Many of the names of things and of officers are objectionable*, because they are some of them ridiculous, and some of them profane.

We notice, in reading the Craftsman, an account of the ORIENTAL CHAIR OF SOLOMON!! This is certainly to the uninitiated a new idea—the Oriental Chair of Solomon! We have heard of the Chair of St. Peter, but knew nothing of the Chair of Solomon until we read the Craftsman, page 89. There we are informed that the Master of a new lodge is, by the present or Past Masters of lodges, conducted or inducted into the Oriental Chair of Solomon, and when the inferior brethren are reconducted into the hall, they are presented to the human being sitting in the Chair, to whom they advance, the Grand Master addressing them thus: "Brethren, behold your Master."

Now this idea of the Chair of Solomon is a little amusing. Does any one think King Solomon ever occupied a Chair in a lodge? I suppose Masons attach to the Chair a figurative meaning. Perhaps it is considered that the persons who occupy said Chair are wise, or sustain a position demanding wisdom. We cannot be expected, however, to appreciate the sublime meaning connected with this ceremony; and, indeed, the idea of conducting a man of very ordinary abilities into the Oriental Chair of Solomon, is too much like a farce to be treated seriously.

4. *Masonry claims to be Divine.*

Masonry not only claims to be very honorable and ancient, but even divine. Craftsman, page 108, Masons sing:

" HAIL, MASONRY DIVINE!
  Glory of ages shine;
Long may'st thou reign!
Where'er thy Lodges stand
May they have great command,
And always grace the land;
  Thou art divine."

This social organization, whose central virtue is secrecy, (for which its other virtues are made,)—which was established by scheming worldlings—concerning which the revelation of God says not a word, and which receives into fellowship all religions, from the Mormon to the deist, and which is full of infidels—this organization is *hailed* as DIVINE!

As the Bible gives not the most distant hint of the institution of such a society, and does not recognize it, one would think it quite an accession to the strength of these high claims, if some Joe Smith, while looking through an opaque stone, should find a golden Bible, in which the ancient existence, honorable character, and divine institution of Masonry should be most unequivocally substantiated. Then they might sing with increased eclat—" Hail Masonry Divine "!

5. *Priesthood.*

Masonry undoubtedly has religious claims of no ordinary character, if for no other reason than for its priesthood. "Priesthood?" says one; "have Masons priests?" Yes indeed, they have, and not only priests, but High Priests! and more yet, we read in the Craftsman of *Grand High Priests!!*

There never was but one order of priests on earth that had any lawful claim to that title; and that order was instituted by Jesus Christ, the Jehovah of the Old Testament, for an express purpose; and they were to be continued in office until the Son of God, the Great High Priest, should make his appearance in humanity, and offer up his own body and precious blood as the only available sacrifice for the sins of the world. Into heaven itself he entered once for all, there to appear in the presence of God for us.

The Roman Catholic church pretends to have an order of priests, but no *high* priests. But Masons, a secret fraternity of Christians, infidels, Jews and common sinners, have instituted an order of priests, and even of Grand

High Priests; and at their consecration to that office, those passages of the Holy Bible are read which speak of Melchizedek, king of Salem and priest of the Most, High God! What ridiculous vanity and solemn mockery! What profanation of sacred names and sacred things! And thousands of Protestant ministers, who will not admit the existence of an order of priests in the church, join in unholy brotherhood a society which clothes even infidels in the mock authority and office of Grand High Priest.

These masonic high priests are mere shows—burlesques—a farce; or if anything approaching the sacredness of that office is intended, that pretence is blasphemy; and any minister who would permit himself to be called Grand High Priest, is not fit to live in this age;—he ought to have been born in the days of druidical glory.

I am credibly informed that avowed unbelievers are frequently elevated to this office, and that piety is not at all a necessary qualification for the masonic priesthood.

To complete the blasphemy, the poor mortal

whom the lodge selects, without theological attainments, without piety, without faith in the Bible, without even a profession of religion, is solemnly invested with the *miter* and *breast-plate*. (See Craftsman, pp. 175 and 176.)

Grand King.—This is another office which does not strike us very favorably, as republicans; but we have no special objections to it, and only mention it here to inform the reader that this is a land abounding not only in kings, but Grand Kings! I suppose we have often been in their presence—their *royal* presence—without those feelings of awe which royalty usually commands.

Masons are not sparing of dignitaries. The names, perhaps, indicate more than the offices are really worth. And probably their Grand Kings, etc., do not themselves know exactly to what the dignity of their office amounts, and might say, like the clown *Costard*: "It pleased them to think me worthy of Pompion the Great. For mine own part, I know not the degree of the worthy; but I am to stand for him." But to us the whole matter looks childish and paganish. Who, with Christian and republican simplicity, feels disposed to call his neighbor "Right Worshipful Grand Master?"

Working Hours.—In the Craftsman we are informed that "all Masons should work; * * * * all the working hours appointed by law, or confirmed by custom, are to be strictly observed." The usual hours for working are "from seven o'clock in the evening until ten, between the 25th of March and the 25th of September; and from six till nine, between the 25th of September and the 25th of March."

These are singular working hours; and however important it is to work, and wholesome the admonition that all Masons ought to work, we think it is somewhat strange that *all* the hours of work are *after dark*. They might, one would suppose, work some at least during the day, and not perform all their labor after other people quit work. But they know best, of course. Perhaps part of the work they perform is more suitable for the season of night and of darkness. The Bible says : " They that sleep, sleep in the night ; and they that be drunken, are drunken in the night." But Christians are exhorted to " cast off the works of darkness, and put on the armor of light."

By this scripture we are taught to understand, that those who have evil deeds to perform, seek darkness—concealment—secrecy ; but that good men seek the day time. And this is perfectly philosophical ; and it is true, in fact, in all cases, unless the Masons, &c., are exceptions. The working hours of Masons are from seven to ten at night !

It need not be said that the same objection lies against meetings at night for religious worship, because at these religious meetings the community are invited to attend, and the doors are thrown open. There is no effort to conceal, but to make as public as possible the exercises. Thieves, burglars, counterfeiters, etc., commence to work when honest men quit. Here is the proper analogy.

A good moral character.—Masonry, in common with most secret societies, requires that a candidate for admission possess a " good moral character." We have been at a loss to determine what was meant by a good moral character, in the vocabulary of secrecy, until recently. We find in the "Mystic Circle" an explanation. Hear: "It will not do to denounce as a gambler, every person who may *occasionally play at cards or other games for money ;* nor him a drunkard, who *now* and *then* drinks a glass of brandy and water; nor him a profane swearer, who *sometimes*, but not habitually, utters a *foolish* or *vulgar oath.*" According to this definition, libertines and atheists are the only persons sufficiently immoral to exclude from masonic lodges. Occasional gambling for money, occasional drunkenness, and the occasional use of vulgar oaths, are not actionable offences by the laws of Masonry. This is sublime morality!

VII.

The Sons of Temperance.

IT is important that special attention be devoted to the consideration of this branch of the great family of secret societies; and more especially as this order claims a great and philanthropic object as the ultimatum of its labors; and also because many cannot understand why temperance men oppose the *Sons* of Temperance. We feel disposed to treat this subject with all tenderness and respect; and can assure the reader, that it is a painful task for the author to lift his pen against this order, because it has, confessedly, a great object in view, viz: the suppression of the monstrous vice of intemperance; "which thing I also hate." And let the reader be assured, that it is not because we love the cause of temperance less, but because we hate secrecy more, that we feel willing to oppose the Sons of Temperance.

It is a common thing to accuse those who cannot advocate temperance under the banner of secrecy, as being enemies of the temperance reform. We have heard the best of men held up to public ridicule and opprobrium, because they were not in favor of secret societies as a means of promoting this reform. Now, this is disingenuous, and we protest most earnestly against it. In the days of the French revolution, a man might have been sincerely opposed to monarchy, and in favor of republicanism, without identifying himself with atheistical anarchists, who were also opposed to monarchy. There is a vast difference between being opposed to an *enterprise*, and being opposed to the *means* by which it is proposed to advance it. We may labor for the repeal of bad laws, without being willing to associate ourselves with a mob, or a secret conclave of schemers.

We are opposed to the Sons of Temperance, not because of their temperance principles; for we believe in the doctrine of *total abstinence from all intoxicating drinks*. We know that *total* abstinence is the only safe

road; and we would entreat all men everywhere, in earnest and beseeching tones, *"touch
not, taste not, handle not."* "Wine is a mocker,
and strong drink is raging, and whosoever is
deceived thereby is not wise." "Who hath
woes? Who hath sorrow? Who hath strife?
Who hath redness of eyes? Who hath wounds
without cause? They that tarry long at the
wine; they that love mixed wine." "Look
not upon the wine when it is red; when it
giveth its color in the cup; when it stirreth
itself aright; for at the last it biteth like a
serpent, and stingeth like an adder." Such
are the vigorous words of Holy Writ; and
such are our sentiments.

The churches and presbyteries which have
resolved against the Sons, have also resolved
against intemperance. We know of no society which has taken more decided ground
against all secret societies, than the "*United
Brethren in Christ;*" and yet that society is
opposed to all intemperance. The language
of their discipline on this subject reads thus
"The *distilling, vending,* and *use* of ardent
spirits as a beverage, shall be and is hereby

forbidden throughout our society; and should any preacher, exhorter, leader, or layman, be engaged in distilling, vending, or using ardent spirits as a beverage, he shall be accountable to the class, or the quarterly or annual conference to which he belongs. If the offending brother be an exhorter, leader, or layman, it shall be the duty of the preacher to admonish him in meekness. If he be a preacher, it shall be the duty of the presiding officer of a quarterly or annual conference, to admonish him to desist from his unholy employment or habit. And if all friendly admonitions fail, such offending person or persons shall no longer be considered members of our church, but shall be expelled from the same: provided, however, that this rule shall not be so construed as to prevent druggists and others from vending or using it for medicinal or mechanical purposes."

Thus you perceive that the " *United Brethren in Christ* " are a temperance people, after the straitest sect, and that to accuse them of hostility to temperance, because they are hostile to the secret society called the " *Sons of Temperance,*" is unmanly and dishonest. In occupying the position we do with reference to temperance and secret societies, we think we are free from the charge of inconsistency; for we regard the cause of temperance as having fallen into bad hands, even into the hands of a secret fraternity, and that instead of being advanced and aided in its glorious mission, it is imprisoned and disgraced by a production of the night—an invention of the devil.

Temperance is a scriptural virtue, to be promoted as other virtues, and intemperance a vice, to be suppressed as other vices. Who would think of organizing a secret society to put down gambling, profane swearing, or dishonesty? Why then all this regalia, show, and paraphernalia to promote temperance?

I. *We object to all this parade.* It does not speak well for Christians. This show of dress, and parade of mighty names, such as Grand Worthy Patriarch, are unbecoming the simplicity and unostentatious spirit of pure religion. A true temperance man does not array himself in gaudy apparel, and parade the streets with sticks, long poles, and flags, but he goes quietly about his work and labors by *arguments* and *deeds* to reform all and preserve all in his power. This dazzling show and parade smacks too much of popery and paganism.

II. This temperance society, in the true spirit of secrecy, *excludes from its communion some of the very persons it should first take up.*

1st. *Young men* are more liable to be drawn away than persons of mature years; but the Sons of Temperance receive none who are under eighteen years of age. It is a fact that in towns, especially, intemperate habits are formed previous to that age, in numerous instances. Accordingly, it has been the policy of temperance men to induce young men, and even children, to " touch not, taste not, handle not." What must we think of a temperance society that makes eighteen years of age a necessary qualification for membership? What would we think of a church which should make eighteen years of age a condition of membership.

2nd. This temperance society, true to the

instinct of secret orders, *excludes women*. Women constitute one-half the human race, and sustain the most important social relations. Their influence, when brought to bear upon any moral or social reform, carries with it a force and efficacy beyond any other. And yet this Order excludes woman! And, especially in the temperance reform, who ever thought of excluding her until the "Sons" were born? Who can appreciate more clearly the woes of intemperance than the wife and daughter of the inebriate? Who can plead with greater eloquence against the unlawful traffic of the rumseller than the mother, as she sees her only son and supporter nearing the drunkard's grave? The undeniable answer is, *none*. And yet this boasted society, in its selfishness, declares to the world that they can do without her influence—that they can drive King Alcohol from our borders without the aid of woman!

3d. This society virtually excludes *old men*. The initiatory fee for a man in the prime of life is $2; but a man of 60 years of age must pay $8, and a man of 70 must pay $18.

4th. This temperance society is objectionable, because it excludes a class of reformed inebriates, and temperance men who are incapacitated from earning a livelihood:

I will quote here the energetic language of Mr. Blanchard, a Presbyterian minister, from his admirable sermon on the subject:

"Having thus rejected delicate women and tender children, and virtually rejected the feeble old who are poor, its exclusion next falls on the blind, the lame, the mutilated and the maimed; aye, in the words of their Constitution, (and there could be no worse,) upon all "*who are in any way incapacitated from earning a livelihood*"! Thus they punish misfortune! They brand honest misery with disgrace. A man has lost a limb in aiding his neighbor; he knocks at the door of the Division, and is spurned: why? Because he has stolen? No. Is a liar? No. Gambler—swindler—atheist? None of these. Why, then, is he thrust from the threshold of this BENEVOLENT institution? Because he is unfortunate. Because he has a wooden leg. Gracious God! Have philanthropy and benevolence come down to us in a shape like this? Do mercy and compassion pass by all those likely to need their charities to bless those who do not? Has an institution *no* objects but to reform, nurse, and bury us, which repels the penniless, sickly, and old? Or are the initiation fees, weekly dues, and occasional fines the true reason why this Order takes its members from the hale, hearty, and property-getting male citizens, between the ages of 18 and 50?

"I intend no disrepect by the comparison; but every one can see that if a man-merchant comes into a population to buy slaves, he selects and rejects the same classes, and upon the same principle on which this Order selects its members; with the single exception that the slave buyer takes females. And the reason is, that, in both cases, these persons are not wanted for benevolent purposes, but for *pecuniary purposes*, and purposes of ambition. Both take, first, hale men from 18 to 50; next, from 50 to 60, and reject the crippled, lame, and blind."

5th. But we object to the Sons of Temperance, because they have served to remove some of the odium which justly rested upon secret societies. They have done a thousand times more for the cause of secrecy than for the cause of temperance. The glorious cause of temperance is made to conceal the native ugliness and wickedness of the works of darkness.

This same principle of conduct is alluded to in the prophecy of Isaiah 4: 1. "And in that day seven women shall take hold of one man, saying, we will eat our own bread and wear our own apparel, only let us be called by thy name to take away our reproach." Thus the cause of temperance has been the means of bearing away the reproach of secret societies. We object to the prostitution of so good a cause to so bad a purpose. Masonry can now boast of the Sons as a stepping-stone to their fraternity.

6th. We cannot patronize the Sons, because they have divided and weakened the friends of the cause of temperance. There are multitudes of warm temperance men who are conscientiously opposed to the admission of secrecy into the social organization. Now the Sons of Temperance have endeavored to thrust upon all the friends of temperance a principle which very many regard as odious, or practically exclude them from the only temperance society which they regard as efficient. This has produced an uncalled-for schism in the ranks of the temperance army. This has weakened and rendered impotent the temperance movement. This identifying the noble cause of temperance with the dark cause of secrecy was a device of the grand deceiver, and it has worked admirably for him. Good men have been at a loss to determine what course to pursue. They were too honest to love a secret society, and too temperate to give their influence to dramsellers. To many there seemed only a choice between two evils, and thus have multitudes of good and honest men been dragooned into the service of secrecy.

But of this there is no necessity. Neither the cause of temperance, nor any other good cause, is under any obligations to secret, oath-bound fraternities. Temperance has been and can be most successfully advanced in the use of those means which the Bible and sound philosophy have furnished and prescribed. Speak openly, labor openly, reason publicly, and address men as reasonable beings. Collect in the temperance army the young, the old, and the fair sex—press its claims—agitate the subject, in the lecture room, in the shop, in the store, at the fireside, and above all in the pulpit, and you will make intemperance quail, and her strongest fortress fall like the walls of Jericho.

Away with your secrecy, your flags, poles, paraphernalia, and Worthy Patriarchs! Away with your lodges! A good cause does not need bad means to sustain or advance it. Let the devil and darkness have their appropriate means for the accomplishment of their designs. Let all this trash of secrecy be blown away, and let temperance men and women go about the work of reforming the inebriate, and preserving our youth from intemperance, in a rational way—in the way that Christ labored—in the way the holy apostles labored—in the way the martyrs labored—in the way Howard labored, and in the way that all philanthropists have ever labored.

Begone with the consummate folly, that even the cause of temperance must seek refuge behind bolts and bars, under a nonsensical regalia, and the mock titles of Patriarchs, Grand Worthy Patriarchs, and all that sort of stuff. To believe that these baubles are necessary for the promotion of such a cause, is to go back in our modes of thinking to those dark ages when priests could not read, or kings write their own names.

It may be asked, have not the *Sons* done *some* good? Undoubtedly they have; and what organization has not? No man acquainted with history will say that the Jesuits have not done some good. Their labors in the promotion of a particular description of education, science, and civilization, have been very extensive; but does this fact apologize for the existence of such a society? By no means. They are a corrupt and dangerous body of men, and every nation should be careful to avoid their acquaintance. The Roman Catholic church does much good. They feed and educate more orphan children, and attend to more people in distress, than the *Sons* can do. But who will say that we must therefore join them, or cease to oppose them? The doing of some or even much good, affords no argument in the case, because the organization is INHERENTLY WRONG, and the doing of good can never form an excuse or palliation for doing wrong.

And further, it is a lamentable fact, that the cause of temperance has gained nothing but weakness and decrepitude, from its connection with the *Sons*.

One further remark, in all kindness, to the *Sons*. It is, that if they live to be old, (which is not very probable,) they will change to quite another thing. I am credibly informed that they are inventing a higher order, into which one cannot enter without passing through the first degree, or state of ordinary " Sons." This is but the beginning of its growth, and the day will come when the promotion of temperance will be among the minor objects of this society. Even now it is but one of several objects. They have all the common objects of secret societies; but as a *bait* (in charity I speak it) to draw in adherents, they hang out the flag of temperance. To such hands we are exhorted to commit the cause of temperance, and into such a society we are exhorted to go, to partake of its benefits and share in its labors of benevolence—(provided *always* that we are of the proper sex, or are not too old or too young, or in *any* way incapacitated to earn a livelihood!) We can't go. We have work enough outside and room enough to do it in, and for the present we will remain where we are; and we warn young men everywhere to reflect calmly, and examine the *merits* of every society before they join, and especially of those organizations which "*love darkness rather than light.*"

VIII.

Benevolence of Secret Societies.

ALL secret societies are either very benevolent or very sounding in their professions, for this theme is continually upon their lips. You cannot converse with a member of any of these orders, without hearing something about their unprecedented charitableness. Eloquently and perseveringly do they insist that they are *the* benevolent societies of the world, and that there are scarcely any others worthy of the name. And this one fact or falsehood—their benevolence —is used as an incontrovertible argument in all cases, and is deemed sufficiently conclusive to silence all objections and cover all defects.

We beg leave to suggest that this perpetual vaunting of their own merits sounds rather egotistical, and the advice of the wise man might be attended to with some degree of profit—"Let another man praise thee, and not thine own mouth."

I cannot speak very much from observation on this point, having never seen a case of real distress relieved by any secret order; though I have seen many such cases relieved by the spontaneous benevolence of the community, or by the civil officer. The reason of this is found in the fact, that a very large majority of those persons who need help do not, and never can, belong to such societies. As will be seen hereafter, their regulations are designed to prevent the admission of all persons who are likely to need assistance of this kind ; we conclude, therefore, that all the credit due these orders is claimed, and much more.

It is proper to remark here, that, even admitting the genuineness of the benevolence of secret societies to members of their own order, this constitutes not a sufficient apology for the admission of the unhappy principle of secrecy into the social organization;— benevolence may be put on as a garb to hide the deformity of its nature, and conceal the innate controlling selfishness. We know the *lambskin* of pretended innocence and benevolence is put on to conceal institutions which are wolfish at heart. And the fact that a wolf wears a sheep's clothing, forms no apology for his admission to the fold. The most black-hearted infidelity which has ever been promulgated, has assumed the garb of superior benevolence.

It is our object, in this chapter, candidly to examine the claims of secret societies to benevolence. And as this is a main point in the arguments of all the advocates of secrecy, we shall be pleased if special attention is given to it.

From an examination of the constitutions of the principal societies of the kind, I have been forced to the conclusion that they are not benevolent at all, but that they are exceedingly selfish. The reasons are found in the following facts:

I. They debar from their societies all persons who are likely to need assistance, or charities.

II. Their charities are confined to the members and families of their own order.

III. The person who receives a charity, receives *his own* money usually, or *bought* assistance.

If these positions are correct, then no man who understands the meaning of words, will call secret societies benevolent institutions. We proceed to sustain the positions or *facts* stated; and—

I. *They debar from their societies all persons who are likely to need charities.*

As conclusive and fair evidence, we quote from their published *conditions* of membership.

Masonry speaks thus in the Craftsman, page 217: A man who would become a Mason, is to be "*free-born*, * * with an estate, office, trade, or some visible way of acquiring an honest livelihood. * * * Every person desiring admission must be *upright in body*, not *deformed or dismembered* at the time of making; but of *whole and active limbs*, as a man ought to be."

To be a Mason, then, three things at least

are requisite : 1. To be *free-born*. 2. To have means of making a living. 3. To have an upright, unmaimed body.

One who was born a slave, or is blind, decrepit, unable to live without charity, or who had lost an arm or a leg, therefore, could not become a Mason.

Odd Fellows require that a person be "of good moral character, industrious habits, and possessed of some *known reputable means of support, and free from all infirmity and disease.* He must also be over twenty-one and under forty-five years of age."

The pre-requisites of admission among the Sons are about the same, though their rules are not so well executed, and they do often take in persons who would not be admitted by the rules. It is probable, however, that much more rigidness will be observed in the Temple of Honor, which is likely to supersede the Sons.

The National Division of the United States declares that no person can be admitted, " who is in any way incapacitated from earning a livelihood."

The above quotations are fairly made from their own published conditions of membership, and THEY ARE FAIR EXPONENTS OF THE BENEVOLENCE OF SECRET SOCIETIES. They sustain most clearly the first fact, viz: that all persons who are likely to need assistance are excluded. It cannot be said with any degree of propriety that a man who is healthy and has some substantial means of earning a livelihood, is *likely* to need charities. He *may* need them, but it is not probable that he will. Not one such person in ten thousand becomes a proper object of charity. The common objects of charity are those who have some natural defect of body or mind, or who have suffered the loss of sight or a limb, or who have no trade or reputable means of support, or who are old. These are the persons who are likely to need charities, and these are the very persons who are forbidden entrance into these orders which claim preëminent benevolence.

He who would unite with one of these orders must give evidence that he is not likely to become a charge.

If a man be ever so virtuous and industrious, yet if misfortune has laid upon him her afflicting hand, and rendered it probable that he will not be able long to sustain his burden alone, when he turns to these societies and asks admission, he is coldly informed by our sublime philanthropists that he has no visible means of support—that he is out of health—and therefore cannot be admitted. You are too poor, and with us your poverty is an insuperable objection. All who come into our lodges must have some visible means of support. We are a society full of heaven-born benevolence, you must remember! Go, poor man! and tell your wife and children that *we* are the widow's friend, the orphan's guardian —angels of mercy to the sufferer; but we can do nothing for you or them, because you have no visible means of support!

But there is a class of unfortunate human beings who are deprived of some of their senses or limbs. They are blind, decrepit, or deformed. Now what do these societies, so preëminently benevolent, do for this class of the human race? Surely their warmest sympathies will be stirred in their behalf. But ah! nothing of this. All these unfortunate beings are shut out, because of their misfortunes. And still these societies claim preëminent benevolence, and talk about being eyes to the blind, and feet to the lame. Ah! they have no feeling for men on crutches. These are facts, and they ought to be known and published with trumpet tongues, in contradiction to the false pretentions of benevolence so vauntingly put forth. They select the healthy prosperous citizens of the land, and exclude all who are likely to need assistance. Are these evidences of benevolence? Rather are they proofs of sordid selfishness.

We live in C——. Sickness is approaching. We expect a time of great distress, especially among the poorer classes. Now suppose the men of property and thrift combine together to form a mutual aid society to continue during the anticipated distress. And suppose, further, that all in the town who are most likely to need assistance are excluded. Suppose the blind, the lame, the decrepit and aged are debarred—the man who is pining away with consumption or dropsy they will not receive. What would community think of such a society? Would they call it a benevolent society? If they wished to abuse language they might. Common sense would pronounce such a society a most selfish and unmanly combination. For these men of thrift to say, we will now take care of ourselves, and all you poor needy wretches, and you day laborers who have no visible means of support may take care of yourselves, is an exhibition of the most sordid selfishness. Still they insist, we are benevolent. Our motto is—Friendship, Love and Truth. A benevolent society to take care of the healthy, wealthy, well-doing citizens! Before this fact all their pretensions to benevolence vanish like smoke.

II. *Their charities are confined to the members of their own order.*

We rest this statement upon their published constitutions, which make no provisions for any save members of their own order. The boasted philanthropy of these societies, like the ancient priest and Levite,

passes by on the other side, unless the sufferer can give a password, sign, or token, in
evidence that he is one of the "initiated."
This is not benevolence, by any means.
True Christian benevolence, on the contrary,
is the good Samaritan who helps the distressed because they are men in distress.
This is plea enough, argument enough, to
open his heart and unlock its treasures. It
does not ask for a grip, or sign, or password
secretly kept. Its sign is, *a brother in distress*. Its password is, *evidence of want*. It
would feel itself disgraced by asking, is the
distressed a member of our order, of our
church, of our fraternity—has he paid his
dues? True benevolence is benevolent to
all, and he who loves charity at all loves it
for all.

But secret societies only profess to help
the members of their own order, which
proves that there is no benevolence about
them, after all their boasting. It may be
said that the members of these societies are
liberal to the needy in general. We admit
that this may be true of some individuals,

but it is not owing to the principles of the
order.

III. *The person who receives a charity usually receives his own money, or bought assistance.*

If this is a fact, it will then appear as
clear as the sun, that secret societies are not
benevolent, even to the members of their
own orders.

In view of the money which they individ-
ually throw into the common treasury, and of
the attention to the sick which they obligate
themselves to bestow, they have a RIGHT to
draw from that treasury, &c., for they only
ask and receive WHAT THEY HAVE PAID FOR.
They receive no charity at all, and to call
it that, is to misname it.

If a man pays twenty dollars per annum
to an insurance company, to have his residence insured against fire, and that house is
destroyed, does he receive from that company
a charity, when he is paid the value of his
house? Not at all. Such companies make
no claims to benevolence. But they might
put in even a stronger claim to this character
than any secret association.

Take a case. A life insurance company, for less than some initiation fees, insures a man's life for $2,000. That man, in a few months, dies, and his widow and children are rendered comfortable with the insurance money. Now has this company a right to parade this as an act of benevolence? Yet if a secret society buries a man who has been contributing to its treasury for half a life time, and gives a few dollars to his wife, it is declared and trumpeted to the ends of the earth, as an act of godlike benevolence.

But insurance companies have even a better right to the character of benevolent societies, for they will insure any man's property. If I put into a secret society two hundred dollars, to be untouched by me or my family, if I have prosperity; shall any man say that I receive charity, when, in adversity, half of this—all of it, or ten times as much, is given to me or my family? And yet, after a man has paid into a common treasury from ten to fifty dollars per annum, for ten or fifty years, and at his decease is decently buried and his widow made the recipient of a little relief, perhaps the tenth of what her husband has actually paid over, this is paraded as evidence of the heavenly, sublime, unprecedented benevolence of secret societies. The world is astounded at the amazing announcement! They cannot tell how such superhuman kindness can exist in houses of clay! But even a casual observation reveals the undoubted fact that a good insurance company is more benevolent—that secret societies are practicing a grand imposition on the credulous public, and that their amazing benevolence to the members of their own order is based on dollars and cents advanced! That is, if you pay initiation fees, and your quarterly, monthly, or weekly dues as long as you live, you shall, if you need, in return, receive charities!

We have now seen that secret societies exclude from their lodges and charities the poor, the maimed, and the blind, because they are likely to need assistance; the very persons whom a charitable institution gathers in. Secondly, that these orders are as exclusive, in the application of what they call

their alms, as an insurance company; only
giving to those who have paid fees, dues, and
stand in regular connection with the brotherhood. And thirdly, that the bestowment of
money on their own needy members is not
benevolence, as it is vauntingly paraded, but
simple, sheer justice—as much so as the payment made by an insurance company. All
this talk about benevolence is mere dust and
smoke, designed to deceive superficial ob-
servers. The next time they tell you, my
friend, of their great benevolence, ask them
why they are not willing to take into their
society Mr. A., the cripple, when only a few
weeks since they received with so much
pleasure Mr. B., the banker? Mr. A. is acknowledged to be a very honest and pious
man; while Mr. B. shaves very sharply,
swears when he is mad, and, if he believes
anything in religion, is a Universalist. If
they answer you correctly, they will say, because Mr. A. is poor and is a cripple;—Mr.
B. is rich. Still this is a benevolent society;
very anxious to take care of thriving mechanics, merchants, and bankers, but passing

by cripples, blind men, and all others who are in any way " incapacitated to earn a livelihood." The truth is, these societies (I speak now especially of Masons and Odd Fellows) seek for the very opposite class of persons to those which true benevolence would prompt them to look after.

The whole spirit of these societies stands in direct opposition to the spirit of the Gospel. We were forcibly struck with the truth of this remark, in reading the. following extract from a journal which was rejoicing in the success of the order of Freemasons. The writer says: " And now all the men high in honor, office and power, belong to their fraternity."

Now observe, the very men this order boasts of and delights to honor, are, in general, neglecters of the great salvation. Very few men high in honor, office and power, are eminent in virtue, or virtuous at all. How rarely can you find a man of this class who is devotedly pious!

In order to exhibit the contrast between the benevolent spirit of Christianity and the spirit of secret societies, we will place in juxtaposition two statements, indicative of two opposite spirits:

1. "And now all the men high in honor, office and power, belong to their fraternity." (*Masonry.*)

2. "For ye see your calling, brethren: how that not many wise men after the flesh, not many mighty, not many noble, are called." (*Paul.*)

Sentences could not be placed together, which would convey an idea of two classes of men more directly opposite in character. And the *spirit* of these sentences is directly opposite. The first is vain and worldly; the second is meek and heavenly. The one breathes the words which a heart inflated with worldliness would naturally produce,— the other, the mind that was in Christ.

Men great in honor, office and power, find no difficulty in the way of admittance to these societies, for they are not required to humble themselves;—the way is beautifully paved with gold. No self-renunciation is demanded.

Has it ever been said : " How hardly shall they that have riches enter into a secret society?" Never. But it can be truly said: " How hardly shall they that are poor enter therein; 'for it is easier for a camel to go through the eye of a needle,' than for a man ' who is in any way incapacitated from earning a livelihood,' to enter into a secret society." Against such, the door is bolted and barred forever.

Why this contrast between the benevolence of Christianity, and that of secrecy? Because Christianity is from heaven, and secrecy from men. The former came from the benevolent soul of the Son of God, who loved the poor and unfortunate, and never flattered or fawned upon the aristocratic and powerful; while secret societies love and make men worldly and selfish. Christ loved men; secret societies love money. Secret societies flatter the proud and wealthy, and delight in titles and honors; while Christianity says: " How can ye believe who receive honor from men ?" and " How hardly shall they that have riches enter into the kingdom of heaven." Is not the contrast too glaring and obvious to be disputed?

As it regards the fidelity of secret societies to the pledge that they will assist each other when needy, we cannot, as before remarked, say much. As has been shown, such cases are rare, owing to the rules of exclusion. I have lived in C——— one year, and in that time two men have appeared before the public to ask alms; they were both members of secret societies, and in good standing. And there are, in this same town, old and rich lodges of the orders to which they belonged. Why they were suffered to beg, we cannot tell. This fact serves to show, that even to their own members, whom they have drained of fees, dues, &c., for years, they do not always act with simple *justice*. One of the men alluded to was a Royal Arch Mason.

The human heart is naturally selfish, and seeks its own, and it is not in the power of any secret society to change that heart. It is impossible, by the simple "initiation" of a man to give him a warm and benevolent spirit. Selfishness is at the root of all sin,

and, therefore, is deeply seated and firmly
fixed in the soul. Secret societies have no
provision for the removal of that innate
wickedness. They have no Christ to offer,
no plan of salvation, no throne of grace, and
therefore are powerless to change and renew
the heart. And by a combination of selfish
hearts it cannot be expected that the aggre-
gate will be an improvement upon the com-
ponent individual parts. The selfishness of
the heart cannot be eradicated by association.
It can only be done by the divinely appointed agency: "Ye must be BORN AGAIN,"
and that power secrecy disregards. It is
not, therefore, a matter of astonishment that
the professions of benevolence on the part of
its votaries are empty and false, and that
even their efforts to constitute themselves
benevolent are abortive.

It is offensive to God to commence and
conduct an institution for moral reform, without complying with his published requirements, and without humbly imploring the
atonement of his Son and the regeneration
of his Spirit. It is, we repeat, offensive to

God, for sinful beings, sustaining the relation we do to Him, to attempt self-reformation in their own strength, and irrespective of his all-wise plan for changing the heart; and, therefore, there is no cause for marvel if such efforts become vast engines of evil.

In conclusion of this part of our subject, let it be borne in mind, that we have said not a word nor harbored a thought, in disparagement of the genuine benevolence of *individuals* connected with secret societies. Many such there are, we are well assured, who are noble specimens of the most disinterested benevolence; but they are so, in spite of their system, and not as the consequence of it. All its *legitimate* tendencies and fruits are directly the reverse.

IX.

Christian Charity.

IT will be proper to devote some further attention to the subject of *Christian charity*, as developed in acts of kindness to the needy, the sick, the widow, and the fatherless. Although charity, in this sense, is to be distinguished from religion, yet it is an invariable fruit of pure religion.

No principle is more clearly developed than the *benevolence* of true Christianity. Christ is an example of the most perfect charity. His was a life of charity. The care of the Redeemer was incessantly bestowed upon the distressed, and his sympathies were ever with the humble and indigent. He was no fawning flatterer of aristocracy, licking the hand of wealth and power. No, thank heaven! He was a friend to the friendless. His was a mission of good will to the poor. On one occasion he spake a parable, which most beautifully illustrates the character of that Christian charity which he enjoins on all his followers. No sincere seeker after truth will be offended at finding the parable quoted entire:

"And Jesus answering said, A certain man went down from Jerusalem to Jericho, and fell among thieves, who stripped him of his raiment, and wounded him, and departed, leaving him half dead. And by chance there came down a certain priest that way; and when he saw him, he passed by on the other side. And likewise a Levite, when he was at the place, came and looked on him and passed by on the other side. But a certain Samaritan, as he journeyed, came where he was; and when he saw him he had compassion on him; and went to him, and bound up his wounds, pouring in oil and wine, and set him on his own beast, and brought him to an inn, and took care of him. And on the morrow when he departed, he took out two pence and gave them to the host, and said unto him, Take care of him, and whatsoever thou spendest more, when I come again I will repay thee."

This Good Samaritan was traveling, and accidentally, or, more properly, providentially, discovered the unfortunate man by the road side. He did not imitate the example of the two who had preceded him,—he did not *pass by on the other side*, like the priest; nor did he like the Levite, simply *look on him*, and then leave him. He did not inquire of him whether he was a Samaritan, and worshipped on Mount Gerizim. No. Nor did he ask him for a "*sign*," a "*grip*," or a "*pass-word*," or even a "*traveling card*." He had *sign* enough in the *wounds* he saw. Every gash and bruise was a pass-word to his benevolent heart. He was a NEEDY FELLOW-CREATURE, and that was reason enough why he should help him. The robbed, bruised, bleeding, dying man, was probably a Jew, and they and the Samaritans usually had no dealings. That was nothing in his way. He cheerfully bound up his wounds, took him to a public house, paid his bill with his own money, and then went on, no doubt rejoicing. This is the benevolence which Christ recommends; and to all his followers he says: "GO THOU AND DO LIKEWISE."

Do as the Good Samaritan did. Possess a heart such as he possessed, and let your charity be bestowed spontaneously, as he bestowed it,—on the needy, of every color, and character, and condition.

Now I aver, that the benevolence of secret societies does not bear these characteristics.. The Good Samaritan (on their plan) would first have asked for a " sign " or " pass-word," as evidence that the person in distress belonged to his " order." He must, also, have learned whether he had paid up his dues. For if it should be ascertained that he was in *arrears* a certain number of months, he would be entitled to no " benefits," until such payments were duly made. Having ascertained, to his entire satisfaction, that the unfortunate·man was a genuine member of his order, and had not forfeited his right to the precious benefits, by violating any rule, and being satisfied that he was not about to be " imposed upon," and thus the golden charities of the order leak out to one of the uninitiated,—having ascertained these important facts, he might have proceeded to administer the oil and the wine; with the understanding, however, that the lodge to which the wounded man belonged would foot the bill!

But we are told that members of secret orders are as ready to assist the needy, who are not members of their societies, as other people are. If we admit, for argument's sake, that this is a fact, it proves nothing for the benevolence of secret orders; for these acts of benevolence are performed *independently* of them, and on private responsibility. They can claim no more credit on that account, than the city of Sodom on account of Rahab's entertaining the spies. Sodom had made no provision for any such entertainment.

And so in the other case. No provision would have been made, for instance, by Odd Fellowship for the course pursued by the Good Samaritan, had he been an Odd Fellow, unless he had first ascertained that the man fallen among thieves, was an Odd Fellow in good standing. We here discover a marked difference between the charity enjoined by secret societies and the charity enjoined by Christianity.

We repeat it, and wish the fact to be impressed upon the mind, that Christian benevolence, in its charities, is not confined within the narrow circle of a secret fraternity, nor to the people of a single nation, caste, or color. That is not Christian benevolence which loves Americans, and curses Mexicans —which sends the Gospel to the Indian and enslaves the African. Such benevolence as this is and always has been common. It is a product of earth-born selfishness. But true Christian benevolence looks abroad upon the whole family of man and recognizes all men as brethren. It has a heart to sympathize with the unfortunate of every station, color, clime and nation.

Who is my brother? 'Tis not merely he
　Who hung upon the same loved mother's breast;
But EVERY ONE, whoever he may be,
　On whom the image of A MAN's impressed.

True Christian sympathy was ne'er designed
　To be shut up within a narrow bound,

But sweeps abroad, and in its search to find
  Objects of mercy, goes the whole world round.

'Tis like the sun, rejoicing east and west,
Or beauteous rainbow, bright from south to north.
It has an angel's pinion, mounting forth
  O'er rocks and seas, to make men bless'd.
No matter what their color, name, or place,
It blesses all alike—the universal race.

It is, however, a lamentable fact, that many who take upon them the name of Christ, are strangers to his benevolent spirit, and give occasion for infidels to blaspheme on account of their cold-hearted avarice and miserly contempt for the poor and needy. How often, (sad to relate,) have atheists, even, put to shame loud professors of religion, by their superior kindness to the wants of the needy and distressed.

See that poor widow, carrying to yonder stately mansion the product of her weekly toil. She is pale and nearly exhausted. She has been plying her needle early and late to earn the bread her children eat, and the clothes that are to protect them from the chilling blasts of the approaching winter.

She is now going to the house of a wealthy Christian, where they are surrounded with luxury and plenty. Will they not pay her liberally? Nay, will they not, out of their abundance, doubly pay her for her labor, and thus lighten her burden and rejoice her heart, and those of her dependent children? No! Merciful God! they grind her down to the lowest cent, or dismiss her with the remark that some other poor widow (whom they name) wants work and will do it cheaper.

I have seen an orphan boy in the family of a wealthy Christian (?) who was compelled to work like a slave, was clad like a beggar, and furnished with an education not much better than the beasts of the field; while the children of that family received a liberal education, were elegantly dressed, and furnished with many costly and useless luxuries beside.

But there is a judgment day approaching, when all these widows and orphans will rise up against those who claim a place in the Church, and yet oppress them or are deaf to their cries; and when the testimony is heard, Christ will say, "Depart ye cursed into everlasting punishment; for I was an hungered, and ye gave me no meat; I was thirsty, and ye gave me no drink; I was a stranger and ye took me not in; naked, and ye clothed me not; sick and in prison, and ye visited me not."

Though there are many cases of sordid selfishness found in connection with the Christian name, yet all who are acquainted with Christ and imbued with his spirit, are actuated by principles of genuine benevolence and follow the example of the Good Samaritan.

The apologists for secret societies are apt to speak of their *hospitality* to the stranger as a very commendable virtue. I am not unwilling to allow them all the credit which is due, on this point; but the fact that their hospitality depends upon the relation that stranger sustains to their particular fraternity, lays a very heavy tax, indeed, upon the character of that kindness. It is very important, it is urged, to be a Mason or an Odd Fellow, if you expect to travel; for *then*, wherever you may go you will find some of these orders to befriend you. Understand, you must have your "traveling card," or your "signs," by which you can prove yourself one of the company of secrecy,—then you may expect friends. A Mason who would *rob* you without a "sign," would entertain you like a brother with one.

Now, we do not admire this kind of bargained hospitality; and it seems to us to compare most unfavorably with the spontaneous hospitality which distinguishes a true servant of God.

Let us present here, by way of relief to the dark picture we have been contemplating, the refreshing example of the distinguished patriarch Abraham; who is, in my opinion, no less to be honored for his hospitality than for his faith.

As he sat in his tent door on the plains of Mamre, in the heat of the day—"he lifted up his eyes, and looked, and lo, three men stood by him; and when he saw them, he ran to meet them from the tent door, and bowed himself toward the ground, and said,

' My Lord, if now I have found favor in thy sight, pass not away, I pray thee, from thy servant: let a little water, I pray you, be fetched, and wash your feet, and rest yourselves under the tree—and I will fetch a morsel of bread, and comfort ye your hearts; after that ye shall pass on: for therefore are ye come to your servant.' And they said, ' So do, as thou hast said.' And Abraham hastened into the tent unto Sarah, and said, ' Make ready quickly three measures of fine meal, knead it, and make cakes upon the hearth.' And Abraham ran unto the herd, and fetched a calf, tender and good, and gave it unto a young man; and he hasted to dress it. And he took butter and milk, and the calf which he had dressed, and set it before them; and he stood by them under the tree, and they did eat."

Behold in the patriarch Abraham, *the friend of God*, an example of hospitality to strangers, worthy of the man of God, and worthy of imitation in all ages. He did not ask a " sign " or " traveling card." He did not reluctantly wait upon them. No; he and his good wife Sarah seem to have exerted themselves to the utmost in the preparation of the repast;—and now see those travelers under the spreading branches and refreshing shade of a noble tree, with washed feet, the best of Sarah's dairy before them, and the patriarch standing by, with a countenance beaming with love and intelligence, and you may form some conception of the hospitality of Abraham. Go thou and do likewise. Follow the example of the Good Samaritan, and of the renowned patriarch. Finally, if the Holy Scriptures fail to present motives to induce you to visit the widow and the fatherless in their afflictions, to bind up the broken heart, to entertain and befriend strangers, then go thou into secret assemblies! If the blood of Jesus, if the means of grace, if the church of the living God, cannot open the fountains of charity in your heart, then enter the lodge! But, " Oh! *my* soul, come not *thou* into their secret; unto their assembly, mine. honor, be not *thou* united : for in their anger they SLEW A MAN, and in their self-will they digged down a wall!"

X

Connection of Christians with Secret Societies.

MANY professors of religion and ministers of the Gospel, are warm supporters of secret societies; while, on the other hand, some entire churches, and thousands of individual members of churches, regard such a connection as decidedly improper, injurious, and reproachful to the cause of religion. These differences of action and opinion, have created no little unpleasantness, and even ill will, within the pale of many churches.

The *"United Brethren in Christ"* are among those who regard such connection as decidedly wrong; and they have engrafted into their discipline the following rule or law, viz:
"Freemasonry, in every sense of the word, shall be totally prohibited; and there shall

be no connection with secret combinations—
(a secret society is one whose initiatory ceremony, or bond of union, is a secret); and
any member found connected with such society, shall be affectionately admonished,
twice or thrice, by the preacher in charge;
and if such member does not desist in a
reasonable time, he shall be notified to appear
before the tribunal to which he is amenable,
and if he still refuses to desist, shall be expelled from the church." (Discipline, page
85, sec. 31.)

Various efforts have been made to induce
that church to repeal this stringent rule, but
without the most distant hope of success; an
overwhelming majority most religiously believing—as will be seen by a reference to the
action of their last General Conference, held
at Germantown, Ohio—a connection with any
secret society a very dangerous, because a
very popular, mode of conformity to the
world. They did not view the question of
such connection in the light of *expediency*,
but in the light of God's Word. They had
to do with *right or wrong* in the case, and

were disposed, in humble reliance upon Divine Providence, to leave the result with Him.

The question of *expediency* has no doubt exerted a controlling influence on the action of many ecclesiastical bodies, in respect to this, as well as many other popular evils. Loss of members, of popularity, of salaries —these have been frightful evils, haunting them like infernal ghosts, in their deliberative assemblies, until they have become willing, in many cases, tamely to resolve to do right—*when it is expedient*. And we fear that many popular denominations are unwilling to agitate the question of connection with secret societies, from this very cause. A worthy, popular, and, in many respects, very good preacher, said to me: "I know your position is right—I know that these societies are worldly, and are eating out the vitals of religion; but what can I do? Our church is full of the members of secret societies, and I dare not say a word." Poor man! he was a *slave* in a Protestant American church.

Another insidious device, I fear, of Satan,

is, to represent a connection with secret societies as an *indifferent* matter, involving no
moral question whatever, and one about which
the church has no business to be concerned.
The idea is practically acted out, that a
Christian, after having done his whole duty
to God, possesses some unexpended or un-
employed ability or means, which he is at
perfect liberty to appropriate according to
his own private wishes.

We hesitate not to say, at once, that this
is fallacious and infidel ground; and we
tremble to see a Christian hazard his salvation by standing on it. It is *fallacious*, because societies employing so much *time* and
money cannot occupy a neutral position;—
they must be either for or against Christ—
they must possess a good or bad character.
They are exceedingly active and powerful;
and to say that they are indifferent in their
influences, so far as religion is concerned, is
folly. Millions of money are annually ex-
pended in building and furnishing halls, in
regalia, and dues; a large share of time is
consumed; much is said and done; so that

the plea, which excuses a Christian from responsibility while engaging in this work, is false and deceptive.

* Suppose that a few boys, in the house of a large and flourishing family, should take it into their heads to meet in a certain room of their father's dwelling every week, in connection with some neighbor-boys. But they meet secretly. The blinds are carefully put down, the door locked and guarded, and every precaution taken to prevent the escape of a word. These boys expend, on an average, fifty dollars per annum in these meetings. The father of the family finally becomes interested in the affair, and inquires into the object of these secret meetings.

" O !" the boys reply, " we have business of our own, and it does not concern you to know what it is. It is an *indifferent* matter to you, altogether."

" But," says the father, " would it not be respectful for you to inform me what you *are* engaged in ?"

* The author is indebted for the substance of this illustration to the Rev. H. Kumler, Jr.

"Not at all," they reply, "for this would defeat the objects of our association; and more than this, we are solemnly sworn, or pledged, to keep the proceedings of our meetings a profound secret."

"Sworn to secrecy!" replies the father; verily this is *not* an indifferent matter. It *does* concern me to know how you spend your time and money. And there are about your association suspicious circumstances: 1st. Your secret night meetings. 2d. Those boys that meet with you are every one of them my *bitter enemies*; they would dispossess me of my honor and my home, if they could. And besides this, it is a first principle of nature that children obey their parents; and the obligation to obey, implies the right to command and direct. It is the parent's *right* to say what ought to be done. And though you should propose no bad object, in your weekly assemblies; and though you had time and money to spare; the act of going and spending without your parent's consent or advice, is disrespectful and rebellious."

The Christian belongs to God, and all he

has is God's; he must, therefore, as *God's steward*, appropriate the funds in his hands according to His direction. If, therefore, he employs large sums of money without any reference to the will of God, he is an unfaithful steward. Can he plead it as a matter of indifference? Is God careless of the conduct of his people? Will he be satisfied with a *part* only of their time, money, and influence? Nay, verily. God is not mocked.

But we say the principle is *infidel*. It is so because it denies the command, "And whatsoever ye do, *do all in the name of the Lord Jesus*." Again: Christ requires a full and complete consecration to himself; but this position assumes that men *may* appropriate a part of their means without any regard to the requirements of Christ.

With these preliminary observations, we proceed to state as a position, *that the tendency of secret societies is not to strengthen, but to weaken the influence of the church of Christ.*

If this be a correct position, then it is the very height of inconsistency for a Christian, and a Christian minister, to unite with, or give his influence in favor of such associations. *Members of secret societies are bound to each other by stronger ties than to their Christian brethren.* It is well known that at least one half of their members are unbelievers. Many who share largely in their honors are avowed infidels. Religion is no part of the qualifications requisite to admission into these orders. As we have clearly shown in another place, the infidel, the Mohammedan, and the Jew, are all cheerfully admitted into these fraternities. Now to all this heterogeneous mass of misbelief, unbelief, and corruption, the Christian is bound by the strongest ties of friendship and love. He is bound to aid even a blasphemer of Jesus Christ, if he is a member of his fraternity, in preference to a poor disciple, who is only a member of the church! Thus secrecy comes sacrilegiously into the sacred inclosure of Christianity, tramples under its feet the brotherhood established by Christ, and constitutes another brotherhood, which joins the Christian to the deist, and gives the reviler of Christ a higher place in the affections of secret society Christians, than an humble follower of the Redeemer.

Every one in his senses knows that this must weaken the influence of the church. A society confessedly worldly in its origin, demands of those Christians who enter its inclosure, a regard for the brethren of the "mystic circle," which takes precedence of that enjoined upon them by the Head of the church. "If any man love the world, the love of the Father is not in him." So says the old fashioned Word of God. Therefore the Christian who submits to the laws and regulations of these societies, becomes a worldling, and his influence as a Christian is neutralized, if not entirely destroyed.

Again: members of these orders usually *prefer their meetings to the meetings of the church.* If there is a prayer meeting at the church, and a meeting of the "order" on the same evening, at their lodge, it is notorious that the latter is attended and the former neglected. Straws show which way the wind blows; and do you think that he who passes by the place where Christ has promised to meet his disciples, and goes to a lodge, where Jesus never was and never has promised to be, is a consistent Christian? Shame on the professor who is locked up in a secret conclave with infidels and worldlings, while his seat in the class room, or prayer circle, is vacant!

Again: a Christian member of the order dies. Follow his corpse to the grave. How is he buried? By his order. His brethren in the church stand back, and his brethren in the lodge take the precedence. The order uses its own ceremony, has its own prayers and hymns, and priests to officiate, and the prescribed ceremony of the church is not used. The minister who labored with him at his conversion, the brethren who endeavored to aid him in his religious pilgrimage, all stand aside, and his brethren of the secret fraternity speak of him as *their* brother, and send him from the lodge below to the "*lodge on high!*"

We not long since attended the burial of a Mason, and, to our surprise, the whole of the religious ceremony was performed by a *professed infidel!*   Close by his side stood an acknowledged minister of the Gospel.   Now suppose that man had been a member of the church, as we know many are who are thus buried, yet an infidel would have read prayers over his grave, and besought God to give peace to his ashes and rest to his soul.   This is insulting, degrading, and blaspheming the holy religion of Christ.

If these secret orders are not allowed to officiate as the high priests at the burial—if any clergyman insists that the prescribed ceremonies of the church ought to be observed, they are in a passion, and such a clergyman is denounced as a hypocritical Pharisee.   You may blaspheme God, or hold up infidelity, but if you touch the *Order* you are denounced as a "dragon."   Ministers and churches are esteemed just in proportion as they esteem them.   If a church opens her doors to them, if the minister consents to be arrayed in a dress that would make a Catholic priest blush, if he will bind himself in indissoluble bonds with infidels and all other sinners, if he will give up all, and become

the servant and fawning sycophant of secrecy, then these orders will regard him as a
noble man, a true Christian, and no bigot.

Not long since the clergymen of Plainfield,
N. J., resolved not to officiate at the funerals
of persons buried according to the prescribed
ceremonial of any secret society. They
were satisfied that the show and parade exhibited on those occasions were not consistent
with the solemn simplicity that should char-
acterize the burial of the dead in Christian
lands; that to lay aside the appropriate ceremonial of the churches, which had been long
in use, and substitute the ceremony of a
worldly society, was decidedly improper, and
that to officiate under the direction of every
secret society that came up, was unbecoming
Christian ministers. They therefore felt it
their duty to inform these societies that if
they cast away the church order, and called
upon the Grand High Priests of secrecy to
pray, though they be unbelievers, *they* could
not *assist*, and thus sanction their infidel religion. This resolution called down upon
them the abuse of the order of Odd Fellows.

They were called " dragons " with " deformed carcasses," "self-righteous Pharisees."   Says one of the order: " It will take something more than the narrow-minded, and the most unchristian-like opposition of those who, cloth-ed in the mantle of religion, would place a ban upon it as an unclean thing, to shake my confidence in the *heaven-born teaching* of Odd Fellowship."

The Division of Plainfield met and passed a series of resolutions against these clergy, and, among other things, said: " That their course must eventually cause a distrust in their divine calling, and render their services, as expounders of God's word, and enlighten-ers of man's soul, *nugatory*."

Thus the ministers of Plainfield are in-formed that their usefulness will depend upon the character of their feeling towards Odd Fellowship.   If they are conscientiously op-posed to secrecy, they must be proscribed; they are bigoted Pharisees, and their efforts as preachers nugatory.   Thus we see Odd Fellows treat with contempt and reproach those that cannot swallow the whole of secrecy, head, horns, and all. We know this to be the character of these orders. They cast their influence against the church or the minister that does not share in their heathenish ceremonies, join in their parades, and cry, " Great is the Goddess Diana ! "

" I will leave the church if I am not allowed to join a secret society." Such was the language of Mr. A——, who, a number of years since, was converted to God. He had been a very bad man, but, through the unceasing prayers of the church at B., he was awakened and brought to Christ. His faults were corrected, his family government improved, and all his family, who were of sufficient age, united with him, morning and evening, in singing the praises of God, and in prayer. He was living, and teaching his family to live, for a home in heaven. There was his treasure. His love to those brethren who had been instrumental in his conversion was very great. He could sing with delight:

How sweet and heavenly is the sight
    When those that love the Lord,
In one another's peace delight,
    And so fulfill his Word ;

When love, in one delightful stream,
    Through every bosom flows,
When union sweet, and dear esteem,
    In every action glows.

But a change came over that man. Last winter an effort was made in the village to establish a lodge of Odd Fellows. This man was visited and urged by every ingenious sophistry to unite. He listened to the seducer, was overcome, and resolved to join. His brethren urged the impropriety of the step, urged the rules of the church and the laws of Christ, but to no purpose. He was soon so completely under the influence of the temptation that he declared: "I will leave the church if I am not allowed to join a secret society." He goes at all hazards from the fellowship of the church to Odd Fellowship. He breaks those ties which bound him to his brethren in Christ, and joins with sinners of every class, in casting his influence against the church that brought him to Christ.

And it is a fact that ought to open the eyes of those who love Christ, that the members of secret societies would sever their connection with any church in Christendom, rather than part with those with whom they meet in the secret conclave. Now, if this is not putting the world before the church, and does not exhibit startling inconsistency, we cannot understand a plain case. The only reply I have heard to this fact is this: "If secret societies render their fellowship more desirable than that of the church, they cannot help it—the church is at fault." We have often heard this sneering remark. To it we reply, some professors would prefer the ball room to the class room; is it therefore proper for them to whirl in the giddy dance? Is the class room to blame? No, their vain hearts are at fault. And it is because of the worldliness of Christians that they prefer the fellowship of secrecy to the fellowship of saints. That an association is loved by a fallen heart is no evidence of its righteousness.

"He belongs to three secret societies." Can any man tell his object? He is a minister, and pretends to follow Christ, and he belongs to all the secret societies in town. He is a Freemason, an Odd Fellow, and a Son of Temperance. To-day you see him in the rich regalia of a Freemason, to-morrow he wears the costly costume of an Odd Fellow. Yes, it is a fact! there is the preacher in advance of a Romish bishop or a heathen priest, in the gaudiness of his apparel! He is the same man, however, who yesterday was a Mason. But here comes the same man again, in a new suit! What is it? Ah, it is the regalia of the Sons of Temperance. He is to-day a Son! Three transformations in three days! He has three "passwords," and contains within his breast the secrets of three oath-bound societies. Surely he is a man of extensive information in regard to the secrets of this lower world. But how, in the name of common prudence, can he find time and money for all these societies? They all have their weekly or monthly meetings, I believe. Can he leave his family three nights in the week, to attend to what they know not? Can he spare that time from his family, or from his charge as a preacher? Can he take the Lord's money to buy three suits of regalia, and to pay his initiation fees and weekly dues? And is it necessary that he should be taken care of when sick by three societies, and that they should all be bound to bury him decently when dead? Masons say they are competent to take care of themselves, and Odd Fellows say that they can do the same. Why then does he bind three secret societies to see to him, when one is sufficient?

I cannot understand these treble secret society preachers. They may offer a shadow of an apology for a connection with *one;* but how they can plead for *three,* is unaccountable. I will, with all due deference to their fame, venture an explanation of the *motive* prompting to such a course. It is a desire and a determination to be *popular* with all these societies. It is evident they pursue precisely the course which a world-seeking minister would pursue; and as we can find no apology for their course—no pious reason for their conduct—we are authorized to conclude they are selfish men. If they were godly men, they would not waste their time and money in these secret conclaves: they would devote both to the work of saving souls. Instead of laying up for themselves treasures in the lodge and division room, and having their hearts so much there, they would be laying up treasures in Heaven, and have their hearts more absorbed in the extension of the blessed Redeemer's kingdom throughout the habitable globe.

Viewed theologically, the subject of this chapter assumes a tremendous importance. I dare not, as a sinful man, appear in the presence of a holy God, except as I am sheltered and screened by the righteousness of the One Mediator; but no prescribed prayer or other ceremonial of these secret societies makes mention of any such Mediator. Christian member of a secret society! did you ever think of this, when you were called upon to unite in the deistical prayers which we find published in the funeral ceremonies of various secret orders? How would a prayer without the name of Christ sound in your prayer meeting or at your family altar? You would not dare, on *such* occasions, to rush, thus uprotected, upon the thick bosses of Jehovah's buckler. Why then, on *any* occasion, will you compromise your religion, and jeopardize your soul, to please men who care for none of these things?

XI

Miscellaneous Arguments and Objections answered.

HERE is a class of arguments in favor of secret societies, which are in such common and *confident* use, that we have concluded to devote to them a separate chapter.

1. In defence of secret societies, it has been argued that our Saviour gave countenance to them in the following direction: "But thou, when thou prayest, enter into thy closet, and when thou hast shut thy door, pray to thy Father which is in secret; and thy Father which seeth in secret shall reward thee openly." The *practical* argument drawn from this precept of our Lord is this: If it is right and proper for a disciple to pray in secret, it is right and proper for disciples and infidels to meet in secret, form a bond of union and communion, and swear to keep

the community in profound ignorance of all they do in their secret assemblies. No such extravagant conclusions can be justly drawn from the Saviour's direction. He only gives encouragement for *worshippers* to meet God alone in the *closet*, for a specific object—*prayer*, communion with heaven. And it is extravagance to argue, that because a worshipper may meet God in the closet, therefore it is proper for a miscellaneous company of men to meet one another in a *lodge-room*, not to pray, but to attend to the secrets of an order which God must abhor. It might be argued with as much reason, that because Christ commanded his disciples to pray in secret, therefore it is proper to throw the veil of secrecy over all other business.

1st. Christ said *one* disciple ought to enter into *his closet*, and pray to God.

2d. He did not say that a *company* of all sorts of men should *secretly* convene in a *lodge*, to do business.

3d. There is, then, no relation between the cases, and therefore the argument alluded to is a sophism so perfectly transparent, that we should not have noticed it, had we not heard it gravely brought forward by ministers, who hesitate not thus to wrest the holy precepts of Christ.

2. Every production we have read in support of secrecy, contains the following argument; and, indeed, it seems to be the strongest argument the brotherhoods have, to defend themselves against reason and common sense. It is stated usually thus: "Families have secrets, and therefore the Masons, &c., have a right to secrets." This is another palpable sophism. The cases are not analogous. To make them parallel, you must constitute of the dwelling house a *lodge;* of the marriage contract an oath or pledge to secrecy; and every servant and every child must, under pain of death, disgrace, or expulsion from the family, conceal from all other families all that transpires within that house. If, then, it is right to make the marriage contract a *pledge to secrecy*; the pleasant home a *lodge*, into which no one not a member of the family *can enter*, to spend an evening, or pass an hour in social conversation,

or partake of table blessings, and out of which no word or act is to pass;—then it is right, perhaps, to form secret societies. But honest homes are not *lodges ;*—there are no pledges of secrecy in the God-appointed marriage contract;—children are not sworn to seal their lips when asked about home;—neighbors are not met at the door by a tyler with a drawn sword, but they knock or ring the bell, and the door is opened, or they hear the cheerful backwoods' call, " come in!" Secrecy is no part of a well-regulated family organization. True, there *may* occur things in a family which it would not be prudent to publish, and which are not blazoned to the world ; but these things, which may or may not occur, constitute no part of good family organizations. There are no provisions made in families to keep secrets, unless there are certain suspicious or wrong things connected with their history, actions, or intended actions.

We will state a family case, which *will* be analagous to the case in hand, and which will demonstrate the necessity of systematic secret-keeping in families. Recollect, we have not said that all families have no need of secrecy as an element of their existence, but we have limited the remark to *honest, good, well-regulated*, families. But to the case.

A man emigrates into the town of C—— with an unlawful wife, and a family of children, some of whom have been convicted, in other parts, of felonies. This family is anxious to conceal its real character from the community in which they have settled, and to live by fraud. They have within their dwelling a shop for manufacturing spurious coin, and a place to conceal stolen goods.

Now, to such a family, secrecy would be an indispensable element. The husband, wife, children, and servants, must be *pledged* to each other, by oath or assurance, to keep from all, even from the nearest outside friend, everything that passes. That family must be careful who comes in, when they are at their usual business. They must have barred doors and window shutters. They must make secret-keeping a systematic business, for secrecy is essential to their existence. Here is family secrecy, and from such families Masons and Odd Fellows may derive authority for secrecy. Such families *are* secret societies!

It is a true remark, that a family which makes secret-keeping a systematic and important business, is a very suspicious family. Something must be wrong.

3. "Good men belong to secret societies." It is often urged as an unanswerable argument in defense of secret societies, that many good men are connected with them. The mass of mankind are mere creatures of imitation, doing what they see others do, because they see them; and it is probable that the above consideration has led more men into secret societies, (and into hell,) than all others. "All the facts and arguments adduced must be groundless," says the objector, "because Mr. A., a good minister, is a member of three secret societies!" This is a most unsound and unsafe argument, and would prove even the Roman Catholic Hierarchy worthy of support and patronage. But the eminent piety of Francis de Sales,

and Thomas â Kempis, the learning and holiness of Fenelon, or the reputation of Rollin, all constitute no apology for the crushing despotism of Rome—for mass, invocation of saints, veneration of images, purgatory, transubstantiation, fish on Friday, or candles at noon-day. Must we join and push forward the enterprises of that church because it can enumerate good men in her communion by the thousand? No. And why? Because some of its fundamental principles are diametrically opposed to the Word of God; and that is reason enough for a Bible Christian. So with these fraternities. They have been busily spreading their nets all over the land, and if good men become entangled therein, it only serves as a reason why we should pay a more strict regard to our Saviour's command—" What I say unto you, I say unto *all*, WATCH!"

But, says a staunch republican, can it be possible that a good man like Thomas Jefferson would have been a Mason, if the principles of that order were unsound? We reply, Thomas Jefferson was a *deist*, but it does not therefore follow that the principles of deism are sound. Must we follow Jefferson, and leave Christ? By no means. We follow no man, however great, when he goes wrong. And good men, great men, learned men, are all fallible. Let it be distinctly borne in mind, that a society inherently wrong, cannot be made right by the connection of a few, or many good men. We must, however, in all charity, remark, that few, if any, truly *godly* men, within our observation, are found, who are warm adherents of secret associations. Understand, we do not mean by *godly* men, those who are high in reputation or authority, but those whose private, every-day life affords evidence of continual communion with Christ. A few such men may have been entangled with them, but they have soon felt the coldness, worldliness, and wickedness of such associations, and have silently withdrawn; and have said, impressively, "a lodge room is no place for a heart panting after holiness."

4. The following singular argument is presented, among others we have noticed, by Edward Stiles Ely, D. D., in his "Vindication

of the Sons of Temperance:"   "Who ever thought," says he, "that a watchword and countersign, given to defend a military encampment, were dangerous things, unless they should get into the possession of the enemy?   And to prevent this, it is well that they should be frequently changed."

This argument is good, if it is proper for secret societies to occupy a hostile position to the rest of mankind, similar to the position of a hostile army.. If they are to prey upon the community, who are uninitiated, and take advantage of them, then the learned Dr's argument is sound.

5. "Cabinets must have secrets in conducting their diplomatic relations."   This remark is frequently made in defense of the principle of secrecy.   It is affirmed, with great confidence, that some of the most important diplomatic relations require the most rigid secrecy, in order to their proper management.   Hence it is argued, "If cabinets have their secrets, it is proper that men associated in other capacities have theirs; and if a cabinet may resolve itself into a secret

society, may not Odd Fellows, etc.?" Without saying anything about the correctness of the conclusions, we shall present the following remarks on *Secret Diplomacy*, by *Louis Kossuth*, the great Hungarian statesman, in his speech at London:

"I cannot forbear, having spoken some words on the importance of foreign affairs, and especially in respect to the city of London, stating, that I believe the time draws near when, for the whole world, in the management of diplomacy, a radical change must take place. The basis of diplomacy has been secrecy; and there is the triumph of absolutism and the misfortune of a free people. I hope soon this will cease, and foreign affairs will be conducted by that power which must be the ruling one in a constitutional government—public opinion. I scarce can see how it is possible that this principle of secrecy in diplomacy got ground, not in England only, but throughout the whole world, when a question of a single penny of the national property could not be disposed of without the consent of the people. How are the interests of the country guarded and carried out in respect of these foreign affairs? There is a secrecy which would be dangerous to the interests of the country and to constitutional liberty to develop. Not only that the people should not know how its interests are treated, but even after the time has passed they should be told, 'The dinner has been prepared and eaten, and the people have nothing to do but to digest the consequences.' What is the principle of all evil in Europe? The encroaching spirit of Russia. And by what power has Russia become so mighty? By its arms? No; the arms of Russia are below those of many powers. It has become almost omnipotent—at least very dangerous to liberty—by diplomatic intrigues. Now, against the secret intrigues of diplomacy there is no surer safeguard, or more powerful counteraction, than public opinion. This must be opposed to intrigues, and intrigues are then of no weight in the destinies of humanity. You will excuse me, my lord and gentlemen, for these hints. I hope the English people will feel the truth of these humble remarks, and that they will not be quite forgotten."

6. "There are good and bad in all societies." This has become a stereotyped phrase, in justification of the union of Christians and infidels in secret societies. We had thought the argument was so skeptical as not to be found in the mouths of any but unbelievers; but we are disappointed, in meeting the substance of it in the labored "Vindication" by the D. D. above mentioned. He says:

"It is true that in our divisions are united men of essentially different moral character; but the same may be true of the Presbytery of Ithaca; or of any particular church in the world."

We acknowledge that bad men may get into an evangelical church, and through laxness of discipline, when the state of religion is low, may be suffered to remain for a time, even after their unfitness becomes known; but evangelical churches do not *invite* the fellowship of men *known* to be infidel and corrupt. They do not make Worthy Patriarchs and Grand Worshipful Masters of men openly profane, or avowedly infidel; so that the cases are not parallel. They would be analogous, if churches sought fellowship (without a change of heart) with those who despise our adorable Redeemer, and make use of every means to cast opprobrium upon his name. How Dr. Ely could have written the above sentence, without seeing that he was giving "aid and comfort" to the enemies of the church, we cannot conceive.

7. "It is of no use to do anything now, these societies are so powerful. We shall only get enemies, and hedge up our own way, if we attempt anything." This is the temporizing objection of a weak head and a faint heart. As well might the objector say, "It is of no use now to persuade men to walk in the narrow path, for the wide gate and the broad road are crowded!" If the same man had lived in the days of Christ, he would have said, "It is of no use now to attempt the evangelization of mankind, for they are all devoted to idolatry! Lay down your commissions, ye apostles; sell your Master, and bow down with the public

throng." And he would have said to Luther, "It is of no use now to oppose popery. Are not all good men Romanists; and will you not get enemies, persecution and sorrow, for your pains? Lay down your commission, and go to selling indulgences and saying mass!" Begone, thou crawling worm of conformity to the popular will! "It's of no use!" That is false! It *is* of use—of as much use as ever. Truth and righteousness are as sacred now as ever; and every earnest truth you write, every burning word you utter, every devout prayer you offer, will be felt to the extremes of the universe! He who floats now with the current of popular opinion, had he lived when Christ was entering Jerusalem, would have shouted "Hosanna!" and when he was departing he would have joined the same tumultuous rabble in crying, "Away with him! Crucify him!"

XII.

Concluding Thoughts.

THE great thought kept before the mind by the sacred writers is the salvation of the soul. This world, with all its parade and show, will soon pass away; and the blue arch above us will be rolled together as a parchment scroll. Man is a probationer; and just beyond a thin veil, stretches out, vast, solemn, boundless eternity. Upon that eternity he will shortly enter, and there will be a correspondence between his virtue or vice now, and his future eternal happiness or wretchedness.

> "Great God! on what a slender thread
> Hang everlasting things!"

Soon all will dwell on high or wail below. Heaven and Hell are not rhetorical flourishes, —they are places of final residence. The great concern of man should be, salvation. The holy heart of the Son of God was hur-

dened with this thought—*the salvation of men.*
The Apostles of the Lamb were burdened
with the same thought. All men are regarded as either good or bad, holy or unholy;
in the broad road to hell, or in the narrow
path to heaven.

Now the church was organized to attend
to this great work—to preach Christ, "warning every man," that every man at the judgment might be presented "perfect." And it
is clear that whatever has the least tendency
to draw the church away from this object,
to confound the distinctions between saints
and sinners, and cause a compromise between
the church and the world, ought to be avoided
with the most scrupulous care. The church
of Jesus Christ is a *sacred* institution, and
has a sacred work; and for this work God
has completely furnished it.

"In it dwells the Divine Presence—the
pillar of cloud by day, and the pillar of fire
by night—a wall on either hand while passing through the waters—bread while traveling through the wilderness—the covenant
between God and man—the shew-bread—

manna—Aaron's budding rod—and God's ministry, to reform the world."—*H. Kumler, jr.*

Many regard it as simply a voluntary society, having a human constitution, with many imperfections, and to be governed by the will of men. Hence its conformity to the world is thought a very trifling matter.

With these views we cannot sympathize. The church, in our faith, is the Zion of God. He is its foundation, its light and its glory. " Out of Zion, the perfection of beauty, *God hath shined.*" " Cry out and shout, thou inhabitant of Zion, for great is the Holy One of Israel in the midst of thee." "And he carried me away in the spirit, to a great and high mountain, and showed me that great city, the holy Jerusalem, descending out of Heaven from God, having the glory of God; and her light was like unto a stone most precious, even like a jasper stone, clear as crystal."

Such, however, has been the strength of depravity in the great body of professed Christians, that a constant tendency has been exhibited to partially obliterate the line of demarcation between the church and the world, —to mingle the human and divine elements, —to bring in some of the idols of the land, or introduce, ostensibly as aids to the church, the "institutions of Ahab and Jezebel." And is not worldly conformity the besetting sin of the church now? And is it not a startling and lamentable fact that religion does not go down deep into the hearts of its professors generally, but is simply hung loosely upon the shoulders as an outside garment? It is made a matter of secondary importance, to be attended to when convenient, or not attended to at all. Who expects now to see a Christian adhere to the "Bible and the Bible alone," as his rule of duty? Who is prepared to allow a disciple to adhere to Christ alone with that holy rigidness which characterized the first disciples?

O! if Christ were to visit his temple now, he would find it so full of worldliness that he would be constrained, in righteous anger, to use a scourge to drive out buyers and sellers. He would find it full of Freemasons, Odd Fellows, Red Men, Rectifiers, Rechabites, etc.

We deplore the worldly tendency of the church, and consequently its connection with those societies which are purely worldly in their nature, and so admirably calculated by the grand Deceiver to draw away the disciples of Jesus from the great and glorious object of their calling. The day of Judgment only will reveal the fearful amount of worldliness and spiritual degeneracy which they have been the means of introducing into the church.

" In the act of uniting with a secret society a Christian places himself in a false position, and the beauties of Zion fade from his sight. His heart becomes divided; he is soon led to magnify the importance of his new relation, around which there is cast a false glare by the mystic symbols of the order, with their high sounding titles; and the simple, spiritual prosperity of the church becomes a matter of but secondary importance. Then follows, most naturally, a jealous spirit towards the brethren of the church not initiated; a coldness and distance immediately arises, and mutual distrust and disaffection. This result from this cause is far more common in our churches than is generally supposed."—*Cin. Presbytery, from J. Potter's Pamphlet.*

Thousands of excellent Christians have been drawn into the meshes of secret fraternities without intending to offend Christ, and without expecting that their interest in his cause would abate; but soon the new interest created, with an entirely new set of associates, a majority of whom have no sympathy or interest in his religious views, and with whom he meets as frequently as he meets in the church, divide his heart, weaken his attachment to Christ and his cross; and finally the communion of the world becomes sweeter to him than the communion of saints. The Champlain Presbytery, N. Y., thus speaks: "They have reason to believe that many beloved brethren, without any intention of compromising any religious principle, are nevertheless drawn by specious appearances into a fraternal and intimate relation with men who neither fear God nor work righteousness. They are striking hands, in the lodges, with *profane men;* ocasionally with sabbath breakers, gamblers, tipplers, and deists, on terms contrary to the letter and the spirit of the Gospel."

How long this fearful tendency to worldliness will continue, we cannot predict. Long was the church immersed in the errors and corruptions of the papacy, before Luther appeared. The blood of martyrs flowed— Huss and Wickliffe perished; but the day of deliverance came. But then another device was prepared. *Union of Church and State* was consummated; and long did this unholy wedlock continue, before a general effort was made for a divorce. And how long the present device shall succeed, God only knows. There are many, thank God! who have not bowed the knee to this modern Baal, and who "have not coveted the Syrians' silver, nor changes of garment," and have thus avoided the "leprosy of Gehazi."

We trust the time will come when the whole church will hear and obey the voice of God calling, "Awake, awake; put on thy strength, O Zion! put on thy beautiful garments, O Jerusalem! the holy city: for henceforth there shall no more come in unto thee the uncircumcised and the unclean. Shake thyself from the dust; arise, and sit down, O Jerusalem: loose thyself from the bands of thy neck, O captive daughter of Zion!"

THE END.